DYING HAPPILY

First published 2020.

Print ISBN: 978-1-915292-21-6

Printed in Great Britain by Biddles Books Limited, King's Lynn, Norfolk

Paper has more patience than people.
—ANNE FRANK

CONTENTS

PREFACE

Life is gifted to us in ample measure. Nature has indeed acted kindly, providing us with a generous donation of time and opportunity. If we are prudent enough, we can adopt a workable philosophy of living and create a simple yet truly extraordinary life for ourselves.

The problem is that many people drift through life unaware of its magnificent blessings, playing the role of the victim, as opposed to that of an instigator in a position of fortune. Clasped firmly between the vices of cultural pressures, many fall prey to their gripping devices. Fond of earning, yet despairing at its expense. Chasing more when less is far more favourable. They live in the confines of others, great distances away from their own. An upsetting and troublesome deployment that leaves many indebted to their own treasure in life: time.

Written in a poetic, spiritual and deeply philosophical manner, the core of this book's focus is centred around the fundamental markers of our time on this planet: birth, life, happiness, death, legacy.

As you thoughtfully read through this book, I suggest you take notes from the meditations that have the biggest impact on you. After reading its contents, consider passing this book onto a friend or family member who you believe would benefit from reading it.

ACKNOWLEDGEMENTS

I am indebted to and thankful for:

My mother, Anna Rosemary James: in not cowering away from adversity; in persevering when met with an obstacle; in standing tall in the face of fear; in being well-mannered, even when another may act impolitely towards you; in upholding quality thoughts; in leaving a room tidier than when you walked in.

My father, Stephen Frederick Jones: in setting lofty ambitions, and nurturing the process of progress; in not becoming distracted by the unforeseeable outcome of such ambitions; in not showing disloyalty towards your eagerness to succeed; in standing up for what you believe in; in not being fearful of failing; in the fortune of country living.

My brother, Nicholas Mark Jones: for not devoting time to, or expending energy on, matters in life that bear little significance; for staying clear of malicious gossip and trivial discussions; for your detachment from desire in wanting more; for not withdrawing yourself from your instinctive nature, and for not being weak-willed toward any undertakings which may lead you astray from your logical constitution; for your assertiveness in self before laying judgement upon or aiming to understand others; for trusting our country's justice system; for believing in my writing when I myself doubted it.

My grandfather, Haydn Nicholas Lewis: from the moment I was born, you have been my strength, my smile, my beating heart. You have been present at times when I have experienced good and at times when I have encountered evil. You are not just my grandfather, you are my best friend, my sunshine, my one thousand pieces of gold, my comforting meadow, my soil and sky.

You have gifted me with many invaluable teachings: in kindness, in patience, in humility. By observing your wise habits, I have learnt from you to appreciate the rare moments of stillness and quietude in life. Whenever I was facing an obstacle and uncertain on how to approach it, you would say: 'When an obstacle presents, do not deviate or allow for fictitious rationalisations to fester. Go through it.' You helped me to discover my passion in sports when I was a young boy and provided me with the compass I needed to find my love for literature as I grew older. When I was a young boy in school and would rebel against reading books, you provided me with a piece of advice that has stuck with me ever since: 'There is a gem to be found in every conversation you have with each new person you meet. The same rings true with each book that you read.'

The adventures I have been on, the sights I have seen, the people I have met, the lessons I have learnt – all have been made possible because of you. If it wasn't for you, my belly may not be full of bread, my throat may be parched due to lack of water and my ambitions may lie dormant in a bed of rotten soil deep beneath the ground. Many of my writings have been inspired by you, not only by your own literary creations but by your awareness to scope out the good in all that seemingly is not. You have educated me on the duties of a human being: in purpose, in brotherhood, in leisure, in love.

My Grandmother, Anna Sheila Lewis: in not fearing voicing one's own opinion; in acknowledging that one's chosen template for life is not set as a universal commodity; in the essence of true love; in experiencing both the sorrow and the bliss of life in good companionship; in cooking simply, with few ingredients; in the importance of stilling the mind; in the power of choice; in a good night's rest.

My friend, Duncan Kerr Evans: in the importance of understanding that success is built sequentially; in revelling in the pursuit of the core ambition, and in withdrawing yourself from all other ideas; in the notion of 'doing what you can't so you can do what you want'; in eliminating all distractions that may steer you off course during your worldly pursuit; in essentialism; in deep and uninterrupted work; in maintaining buoyancy when the current of life proves too strong; in commemorating the loss of a loved one but to not allow the loss to govern you with an absent mind or a motionless body; in remembering your name in times of fame; in reminding yourself of your roots when money, recognition and power is present; in being patient and wise in moments of impulse; in the gift of unfiltered conversation; in the true value of friendship; in the profit of humour.

My friend, Michael Huw Beynon: in the art of human transformation, from inner turmoil to inner peace; in the courage of forging one's own path – in work, relationships, migration to new lands; in confidence that one is never too old to change direction in life; in acquiring specific knowledge for a particular subject; in unaffected character no matter the cause or conditions; in human individuality;

in maintaining a respectful image – presentable, well-groomed and neatly outfitted; in protecting one's childlike spirit; in laughter proving to be an excellent source of medicine; in time never compromising its duty for anybody or anything; in a lifetime of friendship – from the cradle to the grave.

My friend, James Andrew Noonan: in the value of sobriety; in not abandoning your personal morals, for no human or amount of money; in cultivating internal peace for yourself by becoming good, and in remaining good; in abstaining from the tempting pleasures of lust; in forbidding your ego from governing your soul; in politeness, in composure, in generosity; in treating all of Mother Nature's creations equally; in making kindness who you are, not merely an extension of who you wish to become; in the art of simple living; in conducting yourself in a gracious manner, and with a calm temperament; in regulating a heightened degree of awareness for all that surrounds you; in understanding that all the universe's creations are as one; in not edging God out; in priding yourself on maintaining good orderly direction in your everyday endeavours.

My friend, Michael James Watson: in deep-rooted friendship, whether the physical distance be short or stretched; in knowing your friends as well as you know yourself; in the love of family; in gratitude for an able body and a non-fragile mind; in the importance of self-study; in the effectiveness of a stringent daily schedule; in the ability of fair-minded thinking; in listening to your heart; in remembering that a fall presents an opportunity to rise; in gentleness, piety, civility, and in the beauty of living a frugal life; in the equality of all living things; in protecting your time as much as you would your newborn child; in not befriending wickedness; in freeing yourself from the shackles of material gain; in educating yourself on the rules of money; in remaining loyal to your destiny the same as a patriot would his country.

My friend, Benjamin Pressner Gothard: in having good parents, grandparents, siblings, friends and family; in becoming a voracious reader; in the consistency of your craft; in respecting yourself and all others; in appreciation for the present moment; in speaking in front of a crowd, and owning the moment; in not being hesitant in sharing your wisdom and beliefs with others; in fidelity to your religion; in accepting the offering of love, and permitting your heart to deliver love in equal measure of how you would hope to receive love from others; in acknowledging how you say something is just as important as what you say – writing owns no exception; in keeping a daily account of your right and wrong doings, and displaying honesty in doing so, not condemning yourself by withholding any thoughts or feelings of affliction; in unflinching character; in carrying playfulness wherever you go; in faith and support in companionship.

My friend, and editor of this book, Daniel Bowen: for polishing my writing.

To the Gods: for allowing me to live for as long as I have, and for however long I will.

INTRODUCTION

The Story of Marius Quinto

Marius Quinto was a well-respected individual. Both a pastor and a civil servant. A man that always remained loyal to his duties, no matter how problematic or elementary they presented. A devoted father to three beautiful girls – Claudia, Gaia and Valentina – and a loving partner to his wife, Aurelia. Marius was a farmer by trade and a poet by choice, working tirelessly around the clock with the planting of seeds followed by the polishing of prose, usually on the back of creased old letters often caked in mud.

Marius was a highly engaged member of the local community and a valuable asset to congress. An adviser to counsel, an organiser of many prestigious charitable events, a religious man with views and beliefs only in mirror of his own, a public encourager, and, as the rumour had it, a spiritual healer. Many claim that Marius owned a mysteriously divine scent of gold, whilst others, less favourable to his position of fortitude, often said he reeked of lead. Marius was never phased by any criticism, as he was a strong believer in each to their own with every personal opinion being accounted for. He was in popular demand by many. Never faint in his persona or soft in his ambition, and forever unselfish with his time, he cast his own time in the assistance of helping others. He saved many animals from neglect, clasped open thousands of cans of beans for the weak, and vocalised an array of positive verses in times of darkness. Marius Quinto provided salvation to many women who had experienced cruelty, and shelter to a long line of children who had been abandoned.

He was a man of the people, never shying away from a calculation or allowing a thief to escape the grounds successfully. Marius possessed an aura and a level of intelligence that was deemed rare. Some even revered him as an oracle of his time. A man of such surety in his abilities and such profound confidence in his approach that he would often find himself marking the matters of the future before they had even commenced. We know this because Marius used to announce gatherings at spontaneous times for his local commune the very moment he anticipated a rain of darkness beginning to fall. Despite all of Marius' miraculous and godly projections for the unknown, and though he was a man of enterprising earnestness and unique character, he was a man who failed to properly guard the sweetest profit of all of mankind's blessings: time.

Apart from the many sheets of paper upon which Marius laid soothing rhymes of poetry as a result of his artsy nature, he also enjoyed spending time sailing across the open seas on his prized possession, his boat: Le Art Mona. Afloat the ripple of the soft yet often rowdy waves, Marius, despite the immense risks, found tremendous prosperity in casting the sail of the Le Art Mona in the direction of the high seas. Proving relentless in his toil to bring back the most remarkable and satiable of catches from the ocean's unforgiving forces, he would never return empty-handed. Prior to each departure of Marius' daring voyages, his three young daughters would never cease to cry out uncontrollably for him not to leave. Each holding onto him like his departure was one of no return, never to see their father again. Moments prior to Marius grounding his final few steps out the front door, his wife, Aurelia, would exclaim to her husband the same words:

"Marius, my love. Why?! Why be so gallant in an expedition that is so unnecessary?! The food we're all hungry for is a short tread beside the porch outside. The water that quenches our thirst runs clearly from the tap than leans over the kitchen sink. The shelter we require is the roof above your head and the warmth that prevents us from catching a chill is the log fire we hear spitting. Lead and bark are far from scarce for the craft of poetry that you relish. The love you long for is right here, right now, with your three daughters and of my own, your loving wife. What else are you in such rigorous exploration of, Marius?! How dare you stand there and be so mild-mannered in your verses and calm in your riddance. We have enough, for now and for another one-hundred lifetimes over. What else is there?! Please Marius, I beg of you, don't go!"

Marius housed no fear, bound by astounding bravery and awe-inspiring spirit, but at the sacrifice of another element of great importance. Marius unfortunately understood no precessional measures for the guarding of his own time. During his monthly pursuit of roaming the waters of more, in faith of catching something rewarding to return home with, Marius would spend days on end being tossed around the ocean with no control of his gutsy rod, let alone any authority over his rudder. Seagulls would flock above him, gawking in persistence awaiting for Marius to accept his ever-nearing fate. Marius, on this particular voyage, had been taken captive by the ocean's heartless ways. Sleepless nights, lonely days, his skin struck by the heat of the merciless sun, his stomach rumbling for a crumb of food, his throat desperate for a drip of clean water, and his cognitive health withering away with every new wave that thrashed against the side of his already wrecked boat. Marius continued to gasp for another breath of air with every old one that luckily managed to pass, but following the last of his wishes in hope of additional time, oxygen soon depleted. He then gave in, allowing himself to succumb to life's greatest waste agent.

Though Marius was more than aware of what his skilled farming could accomplish, and despite the freshly ripe tomatoes and cheerfully sprouted potatoes that were constantly calling for his hands' picking, he would always overlook his local crop for a much larger, more rewarding yet far more perilous, oceanic catch. And this is where the story of Marius Quinto ends. His unprecedented surge of motivation to carry out a baron of daily deeds resulted in him self-sabotaging the most valuable commodity of them all: time. And the outcome? Marius was never a champion to himself, never a victor of his own life, but always in service or celebration of another.

Was Marius fuelled by his ego, his unquenchable thirst to want more even though he had more than enough? Perhaps there was an internal void that Marius was obsessed with filling by locating the right fountain? If Marius' ego became his own worst enemy, what was left for his future if the date of his death were to be different? What if he had felt his daughters' tears and clearly understood his wife's message? Would it really have taken such an experience of profound awakening for Marius to have realised the mouth-wateringly ripe tomatoes growing outside his porch, therefore deeming his voyages out into the ruthless currents of the open seas unnecessary? And what about the local community who were always ready to support him in his pursuits? If Marius already had more than enough, what else remained for him to be in such unrelenting pursuit of?

The teachings within the story of Marius Quinto hold a fortress of lessons. Some would argue that it was just Marius' time. Others would be in favour of saying he lived for others when he was incognisant of his own blessings of time, therefore he knew no difference. My opinion, if I could be so daring to add, would be that Marius knew the structures of his rituals just as well as he knew the soil he turned was healthful and the words he wrote were readable.

Remembering that there are no real victors in life could be the most valuable lesson of them all. Everybody owns an expiration date despite some treading their years as if they do not. Perhaps this was why Marius Quinto was so fearless in his ventures? Death is the universal commonality which all men and all creatures share. It cannot be voided, subject to pause; nor can it be tamed, for the hands of time bow to nobody.

Reflecting on Marius' life, it is evident that the human condition craves more despite already obtaining enough. Does one not observe the family and friends that surround them? And the bread that is broken beside them? Is the lining that keeps one warm at night now not plump enough? Converse with enough people and you will soon realise how few are grateful for the relic of time. Some sparring with its profound elegance as if it were an opponent, unaware that it is, in fact, their closest ally. Others speak foul of its ceaseless natural flow as if they were a victim to it, unaware that they are in truth a miracle of it. Some steal shamelessly in its generous providing, leaving few to ever reap the heavenly advantages of its presence.

If you were compelled to review your past years, how would you react if most were proven to be carelessly awarded to wasteful matters? How would you feel if more than few had been famished by irrelevant acts? What about those individuals who didn't deserve your praise but you fraudulently granted it anyway? How would you feel if you wasted many years at the beck and call of hosting other people's social events? Constantly opening and closing doors for others? Pouring other people's beverages? Kneeling upon strangers' feet to polish their already overly-polished shoes? What about tending to a long line of ungrateful tenants? Being bombarded with constant demands of clients? Bickering with your spouse? Fulfilling tasks of others at the expense of the fulfilment of your own? You see, when one devotes their years to tasks befitting of those of a servant, their status of enterprising change will forever be an enemy in their favour.

In the words of Chuck Palahniuk, or rather, to quote Tyler Durden from the movie Fight Club: "People do it everyday, they talk to themselves ... They see themselves as they'd like to be, they don't have the courage you have, to just run with it."

It is crucial that we continually spectate our lives from a great height – similar to how the seagulls were circling

Marius Quinto whilst he lay helpless on the deck of his boat awaiting death to take him – because if we fail to do so, we end up drifting through life in a sort of dream state, never really awake, never really asleep, sleepwalking our way through life – thus never really living.

The story of Marius Quinto is fictional, but the narrative which I have attempted to depict within the story is boldly non-fictional – for this is how so many people choose to, dare I say it, live.

As the economy continues to speed on like a race car looping around a track, it doesn't mean that you have to put your helmet on and enter into the race yourself. There will be times in your life when you feel that your life is not your life at all. This especially rings true in the new economy, in which it is easy to get caught up in the humdrum of daily life – taking on so much so often and doing so much so fast that very little of real significance ends up getting done. For the majority of individuals in the world, as it was for Marius Quinto, this is their life.

"Beware the barrenness of a busy life," Socrates wrote, which is to say that it is perfectly okay to ease your foot off the throttle of life from time to time so you are able to hear the song of a bird, savour the smell of freshly cut grass, feel the softness of your lover's skin, and appreciate the silence of the night and majesty of the stars above you.

Remind yourself: The way forward is often the way back.

MEDITATIONS

Many of us believe that life runs its course far too 1
swiftly. That the passage of time travels so rapidly that
we are left wondering where it's disappeared to. But
within this lies the real dilemma. For it is not that
life itself moves in too fast a motion; it is that we, the
humans, choose not to live. When we dismiss the art
of living and take on the dissatisfying act of merely
existing, time passes quickly. So quickly, in fact, that it
leaves us planted in a deep state of physiological loom
in which we struggle to comprehend where time has
gone. Many people wish they had more time to live,
but the duration of one's life is generous enough; that
is, of course, if one chooses to spend it wisely. What
most people fail to abandon throughout their years
on Earth is the ludicrous thinking that they possess
an infinite amount of time. But we most certainly
do not. Be gone with the pitiful squandering of your
prodigious skills, speech, tastes, character and will,
and begin to feel the welcoming surge of pleasantries
in which you've been gifted. Fear not that tomorrow
is near, but instead embrace all that lies before you
today. For there is no certainty of tomorrow's arrival.

Forgetting that time is a construct, we often trick 2
ourselves into believing we are immortal. Banish your
doltishness at once – you most certainly are not! Life
is long, but some of us make the foolish mistake in

acting like it's limitless. Therefore, the allotted time we have on Earth should be time well spent. Time to relish without the boarding of overindulgence. Time to rejoice in the absence of ill manners to any other. Time to be present without the disturbance of any corrosive distractions. If time is blessed upon our lives to enable us to live, wouldn't the more trivial matters in life become far less pressing? Wouldn't this permit us to live from dawn to dusk in harmonious grace and prosperity instead of anguish and despair? Since when did the commodity of time translate into a language of such wastefulness? When will the rightful hour appear to display its confidence in that more doesn't always represent more, and to demonstrate its courage in educating people that owning less is far more favourable. For when man realises that the less obtained is the more acquired, only then will he begin to understand the deeper meaning of life.

3 We are born weak and we die weak. We are brought into this life as small, feeble and dependent humans. We take to our graves withered, frail and dependent humans. Should we not, then, strive to become as strong, worthy and independent as we can in-between the start and end of our lives?

4 As we continue to age whilst the merciless hands of time tick on, many individuals often reflect back on their past defeats and triumphs. They cast their line of thoughts upon the energy in which they have expended for certain people and specific assignments over their lifespan. And if such past triumphs cannot

be entertained, they slouch and yawn and begin to harness a self-afflicting attitude to why duties were not carried out and why certain opportunities were not seized. They now halt as if time would halt with them. How delusional of one to house such stupidity! Is one not aware that time waits for no man, animal, object, or natural disaster? And when the unthinkable finally becomes tangible, their waking years have already made one too many appearances to inhibit the accommodation of further change. Waste agents have already begun their preparations to march their way in. Therefore, their last supper is near.

Today's lesson: forgiveness. Of others, but more so, of 5
myself.

If a seed is not willing to sprout into something 6
more worthy than its direct self, what use is it? The seed could still exist, despite being buried deep beneath thick layers of soil for hundreds of years, simply laying there in fathom with great potential to make something more of itself, yet the seed decides to show no will. Instead, the seed remains stagnant and becomes content with its false sense of purpose, bedding itself into an eternal state of slumber. The half-awake seed is similar to how so many people opt to spend their time on Earth. Though they possess a bounty of potential, they foolishly choose not to deploy it. Instead, they merely float through the years just like time itself: unphased and ever dissatisfied. You see, whilst man may be granted life, this doesn't necessarily mean that he will act in an advantageous

manner because of it. Those who squander the most valuable blessing of all mankind are not living, they are merely existing.

7 Rather puzzling is the mother who ceases to value the relic of time until after her daughter has taken her own life. Are these the extents that many individuals must experience in order to fully appreciate the gift of time? Why is it only now that the hands of time have begun to show? Now is the light of day she sees only after the passing of a loved one. As an elderly mother matures into her existence, how disheartening is it for her to only now begin praying for additional time when her time on Earth is nearing its end?

8 Do not starve your brain of literature, your mouth of wine nor your belly of bread. Only assign yourself a course of starvation when it comes to your most dangerous enemy: your egoistic mind.

9 How brave of one to donate their time to others in which they are unsure they even have time for themselves, feeling the need to please everybody but themselves! Is this a form of poorly executed escapism? Unhinged spiritual stability? A turbulent past in which one forever craves closure of? A cluster of rejections in which one is trying to gain acceptance of? If not this, what else, then?

10 Life and death: for the day that we were born was the first day in which we began our preparations to die. Or, it could be said: for each day that we are alive is a new day in which we are dying.

We need death in order to appreciate life. If there was 11
no death at the end of life, life would remain barren,
shapeless and scant of hope. To die is to give life
meaning; to live is to give death purpose.

We are alive right now, which means someday we 12
will not be. A newborn into a youth, an adult into
a pensioner, and every generation that follows, all
to eventually lay at rest. All men, all women, and
all animals will taste the flavours of which their last
supper is set to provide.

Many people view death as if it were preying on 13
them, picking them out of the crowd within the arena
that surrounds them. In truth, however, death is not
subjecting you or anybody else. Death is our greatest
defendant and our closest ally. In the words of Steve
Jobs: "Death is very likely the single best invention of
life, it is life's change agent. It clears the old to make
way for the new."

Why do we toil so rigorously and so persistently? To 14
not disappoint the Gods? To enslave ourselves to our
ambitions? To make our guardians proud? To remain
loyal to our nature? Perhaps we toil in the aim of
reaching a destination that is unreachable?

Life is similar to a novel; it should not be critiqued on 15
the length of the novel as much as it should be on the
content within.

Open your ears more than you do practise verse to 16
others and you will soon manifest an awareness

similar to the one in which your higher power possesses. Desire no more than you need and seek no more than you have, so that you appreciate life with having enough.

17 Though one should not scope out death, it is not to say that one shouldn't be aware of it. Fear not of dying, but fear a life not lived.

18 Many people seek the meaning of life – and, in the process, often miss the meaning of death.

19 When a blank shadow casts itself upon your day, it is important to remind yourself that for every shadow that is unwelcomely cast, eventually, and undoubtedly, it will always be reeled back in. For those of you who may be experiencing a concord of worry in your life right now, whether that concord of worry is a direct result of financial hardships, relationship difficulties, cognitive confusion or spiritual imbalances, know that faith, our almighty positive reinforcer of life, will forever remain by your side.

20 Death is certain, yet rarely favoured. Death, a topic which is most uncommon to the non-stoic, does not frighten me – in fact, it excites me. Why should I not be fearless towards it? When death takes me, I will simply be returning to my natural state; the state that I owned long before I was born. Whether I meet death for the second time due to a fall from a great height, drowning in the ocean, getting eaten by wild animals, struck by a cruel disease or as a result of old age, it is all the same. Death arrives unswerving, never failing to

fulfil its single duty. Wherever you are, and whatever it is you are doing with your life, the angel of death will find you and the angel of death will take you.

Tonight, imagine falling asleep never to wake again. 21
The last time you get to close your eyes, your final doze into the darkness. If tonight was your last night to fall asleep, your eternal vacation, how would you recite the years that you have spent?

Pay too much attention to the future and therefore 22
your present will not be.

Perhaps happiness is not found in the laborious 23
exploration of it, but perhaps in the lack of pursuit for it? We all search for happiness similar to how children wish to meet their superheroes, but, in reality, within our search we are often presented with a negative experience. Why then do we expend energy looking for something that may not exist? Those who are continuously attempting to unearth the source of happiness must be questioned as to why they are in such relentless pursuit of it in the first place. Someone who's parched ventures to find water. Someone who's hungry rummages to find food. Someone who's homeless seeks to find shelter. Happiness is found in simplicity; simplicity is the key.

A free man accepts death: be it today, tomorrow, or 24
then.

If a shortage of capital is all that I do not possess, I 25
will continue to live a jubilant life. Those who are in

constant pursuit of additional capital are the ones who will always be searching for a life of more: "I have all this money, but I still feel miserable." Many people will go through life in search of something that they already possess, but their ignorance to their true inner self wavers them from ever taking hold of it. In lieu of this, they fail to discover who they truly are. It is not an abundance or shortage of capital that makes a man; it is the heart that beats inside of him, the brain that guides him, the limbs that carry him, and the philosophy he practices. For capital is a mere part of life, the same as walking and eating and sleeping is, not to be mistaken with life itself.

26   It's not about understanding that you some day might die; it's about knowing that one day you are going to die.

27   Bettering yourself can often feel like a full-time occupation: rising early, reading much, writing more. Meditating here, practicing philosophy there. Eating healthily and exercising regularly. Honing in on your artistry of choice – writing, acting, singing, dancing, sculpting. Avoiding gossip and maintaining well-mannered verses, listening more than you talk. Respecting and treating all humans and animals – and all of Mother Nature's creations – equally. Training your faith and liberating yourself from any past wrongdoings, from others and yourself. Supporting the depressed, grounding the arrogant, teaching the uneducated, feeding the hungry. Staying true to your nature, remaining humble and avoiding empty

enthusiasms. Practicing politeness in every sentence. Acting kindly, loving warmly, sharing generously at every opportunity. Balancing work and social events the best one can. Ensuring you are well rested, fed and watered so you can be of service to the less fortunate – and understanding that no human can be of aid to another human if he is not capable of first caring for himself. All the whilst maintaining vitality in relation with your higher power, your family, your friends, your partner, your associates, and with yourself.

I have learned a lot about myself over the past 28 twelve months: knowing that there is such a thing as human error; trusting in the nature of the whole; understanding that there are no limits to human potential when the mind is properly sown with trusty strings; realising that quality and quantity do not reside in the same estate; and lastly, recognising that there is no finish line to life, as death provides a new adventure entirely.

Unlike a storm impeding upon the gardener's toil, 29 when it comes to the development of self the constant opportunity to progress indeed acts generously. Though, once on stage and dancing in the company of this progression, be aware of the meddling emotions inside of you. Remind yourself of this: when you have noticed a great deal of improvements in yourself, you should refrain from self-cheer and receive others' praise in light measure whilst maintaining a modest temperament. Doing so will allow you to disallow into your mind the entry of your internal enemy and its menacing inquiry. It's important, not to mention admirable, that you maintain merit within yourself just as many philosophers have proven its worth before you.

30 No matter the time of day, the tears you weep, the reason for gritting your teeth or the comical tales you share or hear, the humdrum of life will continue on – unhindered and owning no anticipation of what may follow. Continue on, my friend, and bask in life's magnificent unpredictabilities, for this is all you have.

31 Do not panic nor seek venture beyond yourself. The meaning of life is simple if you let it be: to be alive, to live.

32 Ask yourself: "Would I rather live a long life doing what I don't want to do or a shortened life doing what I love?"

33 Death lodges a boundary around our lives. This affects what we think, what we say and what we do.

34 "It may happen to them, but not to my loved ones or myself." Until tragedy strikes and death presents, many choose to ignore or play dumb to it. It is only when you learn how to face up to death will you then be able to face up to life.

35 If we rose from equilibrium, we should not fear returning.

Writing a novel is similar to running a marathon: it   36
is a long, hard slog. There are times when you want
to quit. Times when you become overwhelmed, feel
sad, lonely and worthless. Times when you want to lay
down on the floor and cry yourself to sleep. Despite
the struggles, the finish line is always in sight. One
must keep writing, one must keep running. The end
is near.

Be towards death, not against death.   37

If you're looking to experience hell before death, do   38
nothing with your life.

Imagine that you were to live for another hundred   39
years or more. Now, ask yourself: "How will I make this
new life of mine greater than the one that is nearing its
end?" Will I seize new opportunities with sharp focus
and pounce bravely upon them without delay? Will I
prepare for death more diligently so I can live this new
life of mine more rewardingly? Will I tread soil with a
greater sense of urgency in my step? Or, will I run the
risk of living the same life as the one that I am almost
done living? It's important to remember that both a
long life and a short life eventually end up in the same
state. Both are subject to the merest fragment of time.
Both a long-lived body and a short-lived body are
eventually laid to rest. Live your life now, whilst you
still can.

Do not cling to the rope of life and befriend its   40
frictional pull. Instead, allow yourself to fall liberally,

calmly, gracefully into the unfamiliar hands of the afterlife.

41 When you were young, you dreamt of becoming a playwright, a theatre performer, a poet, a philosopher. You had your heart set on it and you wouldn't allow anybody to tell you any different or attempt to steer you off course. But today you stand before yourself with a frown droopier than the shoes that wear you, and you give off an energy mirroring that of a shattered light bulb. When and why did you allow your dream to slip past you? Today, the opportunity to rekindle your dream has returned. Are you prepared to capture it, now?

42 What would it feel like to be happy? A question asked by many but answered by few. Personally, I have found a great deal of happiness in focusing on one of life's most natural elements: death. In knowing that I or no other can cheat death, the more common ground I find with it. Therefore, if we cannot cheat death nor can we defeat it, all we can do is to learn to live with it.

43 Our external selves desire objects that our internal selves do not require. Be wary of what you wish for as everything you wished for may just come true.

44 To practice philosophy is to practice life and death. To practice life and death is to live well, ready to die at any moment as a result of how well you have lived.

45 Slow down and take your time: to be still, to be silent, to be present. Human 'being', not human 'doing'.

They say that age is just a number. But it isn't really, is 46 it? Age represents something and has done for billions of years. Age is time: past, present and future. It can be your ally in wisdom or your enemy in dementia. Age is in humans: in the deceased, the living and the soon-to-be-born. It can empower you in glory or defeat you in grief. Age is in the tens of millions of waves, in the mantle of the moon, in the gripping of a welder's vice, in the thick fur of a lion's mane. It is within you: what you think, what you see, what you say, what you do. Age doesn't define a human, an animal or an object, but it does mean something. Ask yourself: "When I recite my spent years, what does my age say about me?"

This morning could have been your last rise, this 47 evening could be your final sleep.

Many people are floating in future thought as opposed 48 to swimming in the present. Their thoughts, on tomorrow. Their verses, on tomorrow. Their actions, on tomorrow. They ghost their today due to always projecting their time and energy on the future – or equally as defeating, brooding on the past. Therefore, they never give themselves a chance to live.

We often float through life with the illusion that we 49 have an infinite amount of time. Now is the time to put this foolish way of thinking to rest. We are here right now at this very moment, which means our entities are ageing. If you're reading this, it means you made it through last night successfully. But now pause for a brief moment and tickle yourself with the notion that today is another day and tonight is another night. Now is the best time to do something with your life, as time and energy is wasted on reflecting back on the past and attempting to scope out the future. Too many of us hold out for a future that may not ever arrive.

50   We were not born into this world to feel nice, to look pretty, or to live in comfort. We were born into this world to be challenged, to see how much we can endure. This is the battle of life, and the battle never ends. We just get stronger.

51   The eternal current moves you further away from the shore with each new day that passes, yet you still swim as if you can reverse its natural order. Stop splashing, you're already drowning. Swim in honest company, in the direction of the current. It's the only way out.

52   Whilst you may not be able to control other people's mannerisms, what you can control is the ways in which you deal with them. Each day you will meet someone new. Today, that fellow may be kind, comforting and enthusiastic. Tomorrow, that fellow may be upset, troubled and frustrated. The day after, that fellow may be confused, aggressive and bordering on insanity. You cannot control the time and day you will meet such a fellow, all you can do is to direct your mind in controlling what you have practiced when you do: your philosophy.

53   You fear death? "I do." Do tell me, how is this life of yours any different to what you fear?

He need not worry about what tomorrow may or may 54 not bring; he should only be focused on today. Not even today, only now in the very moment. Yes, I have done wrong, but my wrongdoings are not a reflection on his teachings or lack of teachings. So be it, then, for if tomorrow does deliver sorrow, I will not protest against, cower away or run from it, and neither should he. Even with a victorious conviction, it is true that an individual can remain absolute, tenacious and resourceful, continuing to advance in the school of life whilst serving his sentence. Those who neglect to envisage a routine hollow of artistry when confined to shackles are pig-headed, therefore proving unarmed, shieldless, and unworthy in times of adversity. Man can act diligently in the chamber of reflection and progress towards greater education if he chooses to do so, immersing himself in deep study and dedicating himself to strict application, never failing to advance in mind nor character nor nature nor religion or more in the process. Years entrapped by stone walls may appear bleak from afar until a prisoner lays his hands on a book. Thus incarceration can act as man's ally, not as his feared enemy. And if a set sentence arrives, so will the commencement of an impressively devoted scholar.

Regard each day as if it were a new life entirely. 55

Look, once again: the opportunity to do well has 56 returned. Are you going to seize it this time around? "I am." I'm glad, as you have denied such a richness of opportunity for far too long now. If you decide to have a change in mind, do remind yourself that this could be the last time that the Gods grace you with such an opportunity. And when it is gone, it is not set for a return.

57 The only way to win in life is in the acceptance of the loss of your life.

58 Shackle me, trample me, impede me where you will, for I cannot be harmed as my mind can be anywhere and everywhere but here.

59 Ask yourself: "Have I caused hurt or pain to another?" If so, for a reason to support good or to advance the nature of evil? If your awareness is there now, now is the time to reflect on such happening.

60 The universe has created us as what we are: human beings. We can only experience what is natural to our human state. Similar to a deer being a deer, a flower being a flower, a rock being a rock, indifference to or abnormality of its natural state isn't in question. Nature breeds no component of being that cannot endure.

61 You wish for a life of greater substance? "I do." In what context, exactly: emotional, physical, spiritual, material? "Material." Do the four hearty stallions that gallop so elegantly around your private paddock not count, then? "They do not." Why so? "My heart desires more: ample additions." Have you forgotten that you spoke the same words after acquiring your first stallion, then you lead three more into your stable? Did you not? "I did." So, to what end, then?

Do not fear death, for it is as natural as an infant 62 maturing into an old man, as natural as a seed sprouting into a flower, as natural as a caterpillar metamorphosing into a butterfly. Death is simply a reversal of life. There is nothing to fear. Disallow for friction to roam and provide a seamless entry into your bodily sheath.

You say your plan is to accumulate your fortune in the 63 next two decades? "Correct." And what guarantee do you have that you will be alive tomorrow, let alone two decades from now?

Today I freed myself of some troublesome friction 64 that I was holding onto – not so much the external but that of the internal: self-judgement.

Those who become tainted by their emotions have 65 not practiced the management of their own thoughts. Meditation in ally, scarcity of motion in enemy. Tame the ego but proceed with caution, for we must attain stringent order in self. For an untamed ego is an immature soul. I must refrain from such involvement in malicious chatter, poised action of nonsense, and neither should I jostle with the memories of yesteryears or become fidgety of the questionable events of the future that may or may not unfold before me.

Why do we impede pressure and bothersome 66 circumstance upon ourselves with such religious pretension if we have no reason to do so? Are we not aware that all that is, is merely an illusion of what is not?

67 Think, in the now. Say, in the now. Act, in the now. As for any other time is wasteful. It's easy to get caught up in the time that has been and the time that is yet to arrive; to ponder the 'what if' and the 'what could be' moments in life. But in the midst of all of this thinking, people often neglect the only time we can be certain of: the present. And even this time is brief.

68 "Life is becoming arduous." Did you believe it would grow less complicated with age? "It's difficult to say." Nothing in the universe is as clear as many make it out to be. Similar to our human years, just as history has proved: with age, we become less nimble, our body weakens, our memory less sharp, and we develop a slowness for our day. Life, itself, is no different.

69 Death: the one incontestable commonality that all humans and animals share. No matter how fit, healthy, wealthy or wise one is, nobody gets out alive.

70 'The man of all trades' will not be able to do one thing well. You cannot be a great poet, a sailor and shepherd all at once. It's important that you choose one thing, and devote the life source of your entire being to mastering that one thing. Leave all other temptations behind, regardless of what your guardians suggest or the amount of financial motive that is attached to them.

71 If death is an estate that we all own, it would be foolish of us to misuse the investment we have inherited whilst we live: to do nothing with the time we have.

As I met him I could sense his fears, his polished boots, his nearing tears. He would not speak for love nor money, for he was lost, in external worry. The fears he housed had broken his shell, a spell had been cast, his internal hell. He could not move, sing or stare, only to wonder about his next false care. Recognition is no relic, it owns no glee, for only the aware will be able to see. 72

Many will reject the notion of death; some will question it; others will cherish it. The difference being? The latter understand that death has not been created to act as a cruel mistress to project haunt upon our lives. Death has been blessed upon us to remind us to live. 73

The meaning behind Memento Mori (Latin for "remember (that) you will die") is not to promote distress or to encourage fear into one's life; it is positioned as a powerful placeholder to motivate and inspire one to do more with the time one has. 74

To do little in life, many mortals accomplish. To do much in life, few achieve. I am struggling to comprehend what a life of wastefulness would smell like, what it would taste like, what it would sound like, what it would feel and look like. Years scant of scope provide an existence with little hope. 75

At dawn, do not grumble that without blankets your body will feel cold. Nor complain for lack of slumber. Instead, act vigilantly, unsparingly, inquisitively and boldly. Throw off the materials of warmth, temporary 76 comfort and false satisfaction and begin to ground your first step with gratitude for having been gifted another day to live. Waste not another moment. Quibble not on the thought of any other, nor puzzle yourself over the unpredictability of tomorrow's events. In lieu of such fruitless thoughts, go now and propel yourself into your daily duties, just as your nature intends.

77 All that merely seems, is not. All that is not, merely seems.

78 If you're ever feeling lonely, you could do worse than sitting down in the corner of your room with a book.

79 Death by tragedy. Death by disease. Death by suicide. Death by old age. Do not trouble yourself, all forms of death lead to the same destination. We are as one.

80 Do you believe that your natural patterns are out of sync? Identify the root of the cause, then make immediate and deliberate change.

81 You pray to the Gods to solve your problems, but you are not prepared to attempt to solve them yourself. If the Gods hold the almighty power to provide solutions to all of your problems, why not pray to the Gods to banish all of your troubles – anxieties, regrets, fears, suspicions, desires, and all others – completely?

82 I can smell the rust upon the steel bars. I can hear the guards calling my name. I can taste the innutritious food that is served before me. This dirty plate, this mildewed crust of bread, the sticky floor beneath my

feet. My time to spend some time is fast approaching. I can sense it. The thick steel chains that are soon to be locked around my wrists, I can hear them rattling as much as I can feel them digging into my wrist bones. Though, strangely, I am at peace with it. "How so?" Incarceration will give me time to think, time to reflect, time to breathe, time to read, time to write, time to figure out who I really am and what I have been born into this world to do. "Do you not fear prison?" I do not. To me, prison can become a theatre of thought and application. Prison serves a purpose for the justice system and provides a valuable lesson for the prisoner. I know that my time as a free man is not being wasted, and I know my time will not be wasted when I am confined in the justice chamber. For the time that I am due to spend, however long it be, whenever it is due to commence, will be time of conscious development for what's to come following my release. It's time. Serve me my sentence, I am ready.

You have your meditations that you abide by now, but 83 what happens to those same meditations tomorrow, next month, or next year? They have faded into the gallows on previous occasions and you have watched them disappear without putting up a fight. What reason do you have to show such disloyalty to your self-set daily disciplines? You are not fooling anybody but yourself. Rationalisation is not your saviour in such circumstances. Stop clouding the truth and set out on doing what you have promised yourself you will do.

84   Be selfish now so you can be selfless when the time presents.

85   See your life as that of a marble sculpture. Another year passes, another crack presents. How many more cracks can one's sculpture endure before it cracks for the last time?

86   You work so much in life that so much of your life has become work. The calluses on your hands, the premature grey hairs upon your head, your troubled spine, the blood in your boots. Has such rigorous toil proved its worth thus far? Has such loyalty to your toil made you a better man? Perhaps a more respected man? I cease to see it so. To be in accordance with our human nature I shall not contest with, but when such hours of toil have left you emotionally bankrupt, physically exhausted, and on the brink of death, I find great difficulty in not questioning it. You say, "I work to live," but that very life source that you so heavily rely on is fast becoming the rope and knot of your own death.

87   My body, frail. My mind, lost. My spirit, aimless. The future delivers the ingredients for my life in which will be. They will impede my stature, they will become a relic of what is left, what is to be and what is bound to fade. Argue not with what is to come, only bask in the moment that is, as tomorrow can bring new anxieties, fresh helpings of worries and numerous other servings of disappointment. If your today is divine then your tomorrow should not be in thought.

All of today's hours should be clear of regret, free of turmoil, void of suspicion.

You think about him, her, this or that as your 88 remaining time moves on unhurriedly. It is you that ponders on the thoughts and verses and acts and plots of others whilst devoting little time to yourself. Escape this self-defeating operation and begin to do good, for you. Do not deprive yourself of who you are and what you want from this life by comparing yourself to another person. Comparison is a disease, and if you're not careful, it can spread like wildfire. So, with this in mind, be sure to tread carefully when considering comparing your Chapter One to another's Chapter Twelve.

Morning: prepare. Afternoon: apply. Evening: reflect. 89 Tomorrow: repeat.

A commune of penguins dart through the waters 90 of the Atlantic ocean beside one another, each hyper-aware that their current voyage could indeed be their last. Due to an abundance of blood-thirsty orca whales circling the same seas as they do, the penguins are in constant threat of becoming yet another tasty meal for the hungry underwater giants. But despite the dangers that the penguins constantly face, they go about their day as their nature intends: zipping through the waters in hunt of catching a few well-fed fish to curb their hunger before jumping onto a safe patch of ice to rest. What is the reason for penguins routinely putting themselves in such a vulnerable position each day? Because this is what penguins were born to do. If the penguins were to fail in remaining loyal to their daily pursuits, they would soon wither away with starvation and die. As human beings, we too are hyper-aware that each new day that arrives brings fresh opportunities for the grim reaper to catch hold of us. This morning, one could get struck by a bus on their commute to work. This afternoon, one could collapse to the floor with heart failure. And for this evening? It could bring the time one gets to experience the closing of their eyes before departing into eternal darkness. Whilst death is a subject that doesn't have to form the centrepiece of each and every conversation you have with others, or with yourself, it is a subject that shouldn't be neglected in thought nor purpose. Treat your time on this Earth as a relic: value it, nurture it, embrace it.

91   Philosophy: what remains when all else is lost.

92   Your tablets are void. They serve no value to the user who abuses the good nature of their purpose. Consume them for good health, not for the masking of thy troubled self. You will not glow, sparkle or shine, let alone admit that you are far from 'fine'. Merely will you maintain spring in your step, let alone warmth in your heart and exuberance in your soul. Continuing to squander your time as if it were limitless. How irrational must one be to contend with the ever-turning hands of time? There you sit, having endured yet another evening of desolation. There you go, gulping down another measure of liquor as if it were in short supply. When opinions are expressed,

only one side bears the weight. Oblivious to your own mortality, you fail to see that a few more slurps will grant the final concealments of your fate. Universe to blame if no mortal is in sight, every other is wrong, for only you are right.

The only fear I have is the one where I am on the verge 93 of my departure from this life knowing I could have done more with the time I had. At the end of your fear, ask yourself: what remains?

Memories: to be remembered, not radicalised. 94 Current enemies: to be forgiven, never forgotten. Future pleasures: to be dismissed, free of desire.

The world is a riot but your mind need not be. 95

Form a present replica of your wishful self. Start 96 today, not a day or a month or a year from now, but now. Bury the individual who puts things off until the future, and instead become the individual who starts today.

Your body may be a prisoner inside this jail but your 97 mind can be anywhere it chooses to be. Body confined and your mind free, wherever you may be.

How are you, son? "I am happy, father." How many 98 coins does your satchel carry? I stare at my father in confusion. "Excuse me, father, but perhaps you failed to hear me. Allow me to repeat myself: I am happy, father." My father looks back at me with intrigue, still like a statue and as quiet as a mouse. How can a man who hears such truths appear so dismayed?

99 Imagine yourself as a number in the entirety of the world's human population. With billions of others out there, ask yourself: "For what reason am I here?"

100 Do not hide your defeats nor be ashamed of them. Instead, allow your adversity to become your university.

101 You are worried about your health, your marriage, your business, you say? What frightens you, exactly? "Falling ill, separating from my lover, my business failing." Have you experienced any signs of these things happening? "I'm unsure what such signs may look like." Think of it like this: before you are presented with screams, you will more than always be presented with whispers. Are you feeling fatigued? Are you arguing with your wife? Are your customers complaining? It's important to keep your ears clean so that you can hear the whispers before they develop into screams.

102 "This life of yours is soon to be over. I am going to kill you." Go ahead, I am already dead.

103 Others may not be in a position to be tamed, but your mind can certainly be trained.

104 Perfection, comparable to fear, is merely an illusion. Reality is distant when perfection is present. In your internal dialogue, in the universe around you, strive for progress. Do not contaminate the air with negativity nor other people with your snot. Allow your fountain of thoughts to run clean, ensuring that you treat all

of Mother Nature's creations with the same degree of kindness that you would wish to be treated yourself.

Today, my life hangs in the balance. Today, I am 105 questioning every thought I possess, every step I take, every sound I hear, every object and animal I see. I stand in query of why I am questioning so much. Surely the Gods have more faith in me than this? Is this a result of my body becoming fatigued? My mind deteriorating? I am in distress. The decay of my concentration, the tiredness of my body, the exhaustion of my ambitions have left me feeling awfully troubled. I feel like my life is running away from me and I cannot keep up. And once it has bridged enough of a gap, it is not set to return.

The war is announced, the battle is to commence. 106 The time is now to escape your false pretence. As the armour is shaped and the swords are sharpened, soldiers prepare to march, never disheartened. The battle in plan for blood to be shed, clashes of swords upon your enemies' heads. Bodies scattered, you stand tall, victory is ours, the result of thy king's call. The march home is cold in thought of the brothers you have lost, the families to inform of those lying in the frost. The castle in view, your king in sight, a flock of doves are released for your bravery in the fight. The arena you walk for the battle you have won, flowers you catch in the face of the sun. You crave to raise your hands in glee for the people tomorrow you might not see. Your arms to heighten in almighty cheer for the crowd tomorrow you might not hear. Praise you receive for the safety you have granted, enemies on the ground, soon to be planted. Yes, my victor, fanfare is here, but do remember, your death could be near. Today today, tomorrow tomorrow, happiness today, sorrow tomorrow. A legacy, a remembrance, above all good grace, eventually leads to the same resting place. So do not celebrate, break bread and drink wine, for your body, too, will soon slip into its eternal shrine.

107 The best way to approach death is to live.

108 Do tell me: why grunt and moan about all of the things you do not possess that others do? Who and what is stopping you from achieving the same ends as those that you speak so disdainfully of? You too can inhibit the transformation that you so strongly desire if you were to tutor your mind correctly.

109 A grain of sand, a chip from a rock, a droplet of water in the ocean: all of nature's creations have a distinctive purpose to themselves and to the universe that guardians them.

110 Many of my most empowering thoughts take place in times where I feel most troubled. Many of my most troubling thoughts take place when I feel most empowered.

111 Do not be repelled by the natural essence of your very own fragrance of fate. Instead of thinking about all of the things you would miss in life, place thought upon the things you wish to be without: the putrid souls that contaminate the air around you, the

business you're in that seems to have lost its buoyancy, haunting memories that your mind won't allow you to break free from, all of the worldly problems and the concerns of what the future may or may not bring. Death provides liberation from all of the anxieties in which you pray not to possess. How do you feel now, then, about your inevitable death?

Adopt the 'anything is possible' philosophy. Similar to 112 the odds of you being born a human into the universe: 1 in 400 trillion. Not only in light of the positive, but also in the shadow of the negative. Meditate on all that has the potential to happen in life. Yes, whilst the foundations of your boat are built well, it can still sink. Similar to being in good health today but getting struck by a cruel disease tomorrow. Your business could crumble, your lover could commit adultery, your child could die. Become a practitioner of the 'anything is possible' philosophy and prepare yourself for the medley of events that the unpredictable future may bring.

Travel to a place of good grace. Not in the destination of 113 a worldly country, but inside your mind. Your personal oasis, if you will. A place of brave commencement and uplifting assertiveness. Become your own spiritual legend. Don't allow yourself to glide in the slipstream of other people's negativity and lifeless ambitions. There is no heaven to be found in doing so. Live your life as you would wish for your child as they grow older: doing good and acting kindly, keeping in good faith, understanding the difference between right and wrong, good and evil, being a supporter of themselves and a supporter of others – emotionally, spiritually, physically – and being the one who basks in the dismissal of any matters that could be marked as trivial. For loyalty to such disciplines could result in a life worth living.

114 The angel of death can grip one by the collar at any time. Do not believe for a second that you can hide from death, outwit it or outrun it. You cannot! Its presence is nearing, ever daring, and may press upon you long before the first day of your future ambitions is set to commence.

115 My deal with death is constantly pressing. Nothing can trouble me, for I already am what I am bound to become: an entity of stillness beneath the soil.

116 Someday, perhaps a day not too far away, the world as we once knew it will be scattered and torn. Farmlands will become barren and the oceans will run dry. Humanity will fade dim and the animals will vaporise into the Earth's crust. And the cosmos will disperse into another foreign legion of the universe. For someday, possibly a day not too far away, all that is here right now will be taken away.

117 We've become so connected to a life of falsehood that we've disconnected from reality: the life that matters most. A virtual world in which nonsense is overly populated and realism is something of a distant memory. We capture so many small photos that we've forgotten to capture the bigger picture. And as we

gape and yawn, lost in a fairytale world of disorder and cruelty, corruption and disloyalty, we fail to acknowledge one vital component: that our freedom is slowly being stripped away from us.

We live in a social construct. Confined to four glass 118 walls with piercing sounds, flashing lights, and where many misguided souls roam. Shackled and bound by virtual chains. Prisoners within a false world of anguish and despair, disappointment and muddle. Anxious as to which app to open and squander our time on next. We sit, we hope, and we wish for something magical to commence that will forever be in waiting. Slaves to a digital master, and to a virtual space in which order is scarce, duty is rare, and humility is rapidly becoming something of a distant memory. We become lost when silence falls and distressed when activity dampens. For a life without technology is apparently no life at all.

I drift into my evening slumber in thought of the 119 matters that may have aggravated me throughout the day. Reflecting on the positives, scouting out the negatives. If there is ever a day in which I have expended time and energy on any matters of triviality, I don't punish myself with blame or allow myself to feel shame, deprive myself of sleep or say the Lord's name in vain; I instead mark it down as a lesson to learn from and ensure I do better the next day.

I will not weep when tides are high, nor will I 120 cower away when lightning strikes. I will stand tall, honourable and fearless. Obstacles may present but my preparation will prove its worth. I will not bow down to values which do not mirror my own, nor will I surrender to immoral ethics that have been so coarsely thrown. For heights I will climb and quarters I will swim, for there is no obstacle that an act of valour will not win.

121 I do not fear difference, only indifference.

122 Refrain from leaning on him. You say that you are fatigued from doing so but have you ever thought about the weight that he must be bearing upon your constant lean? The Gods can provide life in all shapes and sizes. The bread you are given, the horse that carries you home, the blanket that keeps you warm. In my case, the Gods have provided their blessings in the shape of a man. A man who provides when he does not need to and speaks the truth when all others are conversing with corrupt tongues and showcasing their injustices. If the Gods had not created this man, the heart I own would have stopped beating a long time ago.

123 If we were once nothing, why should we harbour any concern for our return?

124 You are rotting already. The worms are already feasting upon your half-awake corpse. Wake up! Smile and be happy about your life. This life that you have right now. Prevent ageing prematurely and being bound to a bed before your time. Do not catapult yourself into a premature burial by abstaining from providing yourself with the greatest healer of them all: self-love. Do not

bite your nails, do not tremble, do not allow the palms of your hands to clam. Go now and sleep a little longer. Take a walk on the sandy shores. Share stories with a stranger. Give yourself time to sit and think. House no concern, house no fear. Allow the world of trivia to slip past your barriers of consciousness similar to how water drains away from your kitchen sink. Self-love is a result of self-awareness. Self-love is the key: in stillness, in silence, in all that has and will be.

Do not delay living a life of virtue when you can begin living a life of virtue now. 125

Do not be distracted by the unflattering practice of showcasing what you have created. If you write in your journal, write for its own sake. Do not flaunt the process to others, aiming to receive praise for your progressions. This is not what an artist does. This is the act of an attention-seeker. 126

If the devil of desire ever tempts, I ensure to maintain strict loyalty to my daily disciplines: reading, writing, exercise, cold showers, meditation. 127

Speak the truth, if the truth is so. Do right, if rightful to do. 128

I may be killed but I will not be harmed. 129

Are you fearful of dying? If so, upgrade your life. 130

Before you judge him or her about their apparent flaws or faults, submit your own thoughts, actions and 131 plots to an audit. Judgement upon another without judgement upon self is an injustice within itself.

132 You chariot your time to him, but what about your own time? Do not starve yourself of the most precious commodity of all because you have not discovered the power behind saying no. Practice self-devotion in equal measure, or more, as you practice devotion to others.

133 Each second that has passed is now in the past. Dead time. Each moment that has been and gone is now in the past. Dead moments. Death owns all that has been and gone, and all that is now and will be brushed under the carpet of life as the universe continues to run its course.

134 Have you ever considered the journey of death may be far greater than the journey of life? We are all bound to experience what is destined to arrive, but we will not truly know how great the adventure is until we take our final breath in this life.

135 If a gardener plants a seed today, he must revisit the seed each day to see how it is developing. If the gardener fails to remain loyal to his daily obligation, he knows that the seed will fail to blossom into a flower. Though, it would not be the seed that would fail in advancing into its next stage of life as much as the gardener would have failed the seed. The gardener must nurture the seed, the same as a mother must nurture her newborn child, providing it with love, care and attention in order for it to bloom into an

entity of beautiful potential. Art is no different. Fail to nurture your chosen artistry on a daily basis, and your art, just like the seed scant of love, will become stagnant and unworthy of anything more.

It's important to find your abode, a place that makes you feel at home. Build your nest well. But do be mindful that one day, perhaps one day not too far away, you may wish to fly away and build your nest somewhere astray. 136

Your life is similar to a fire: you can only light a fire so much before it dwindles out with exhaustion. Focus on the quality and quantity of logs that you place upon your fire, for if you become lazy in the nurturing process, your fire may burn out and you will run the risk of your life becoming cold. 137

My personal take on happiness: to live every day as if today was the day that I always wished to travel back to. To lounge in life's fine moment of now. To question little and to savour the ever possible. 138

It appears that an overabundant flock of individuals are treading time in a disengaged and perplexed manner. Unsure if their years have been, are, and therefore will be, ones of mere existence as opposed to years that nature's intentions set: to live. Oblivious to their own senses, awareness and purpose, they fall astray to the liveliness of what their time on earth could be. And the outcome for such lack of duty and ignorance of service? A morbid existence. An existence that craves life, but sadly, cannot be experienced. Though 139 the potential to do so is in rich supply, the choice in doing so is ghosted. In short, defeat has begun to set in and the afterlife is now not too afar. As scandalous as it may sound, why do we wait with such startling patience for a life to arrive yet may never will?

140   Bound by covert limitations, people halt on the advancement of their dreams and bow down to others' set restrictions and society's dispiriting arrangements. They apply a universal clamp upon themselves, easing the deviation from the original path in which they set out to embark on. And instead, foolishly and shamelessly, fall prey to questionable new habits set by others which are completely alien to their own. They tap to a submission due to its unsettling irregularity. One that falsely motivates them into handing themselves over to another ill-mannered practice: crafted together with wood and wire, mounted by strings and dressed to impress, the puppet is set to perform day and night against its will, tossed from side to side and bobbed from soil to sky by its merciless marionette in the aim of entertaining the crowd. In other words, they become lost.

141   He who prefers to slumber rather than stand has not yet discovered the beauty of liberal movement. He who has the ability to study and teach yet finds it more favourable to gape and yawn has not yet unmasked the value of communication. He who continues to commit adultery but has not yet found true love. Those who allow their pleasures to slip into a state of discontent have not yet discovered the relic of freedom.

Do not ponder on the thought of embodying what   142
you want from life. Embody it.

A vast fleet of individuals believe that in order to find   143
happiness they must take on additional hours of toil
in the aim of collecting more material goods. What
foolishness this is for mankind to actually believe that
we need more physical goods in our lives in order to
create a life worth living for. Those who are constantly
in thought of acquiring material items are on a
backward march. Their internal compass is broken.
What many people fail to see is that nothing material
is required in order to create a jubilant life. If you were
to have all of the materials you thought you couldn't
live without stripped from you today – the big house,
the luxury car, the expensive clothes – only then will
you be able to realise that all of which remains is all
that you need.

Dead yesterday, dead today, dead tomorrow.   144

We seek happiness as if happiness were the ghost and   145
we were the hunters: quietly, strategically, carefully.
Do tell me, how many years of hunting has it taken
for you to find your ghost? The more consistent you
are in your hunt the less successful your hunt proves.
Perhaps the thrill of a ghost-hunt is not found in the
sighting of the ghost itself, but more so in the hunt for
it. Your ghost may not ever appear, but it will forever
keep you curious, on your toes, on the cusp of getting
a glimpse. So, without any guarantee of ever sighting
your ghost, it's important that you find enjoyment in
your hunt for it.

146 Struggle is paramount in the attainment of our successes. The school of life can indeed provide some tough lessons, but if we fail to grasp the importance of the adversities we experience leading up to what we wish for, the result will often yield diminishing returns. Today a problem, tomorrow a solution.

147 Life can be hard work. Life can require hard work, too. It is not merely about the work that we put in at this very moment as much as it is about the work that we are prepared to put in over the long haul.

148 Whatever you're doing, however you're doing it, wherever you're doing it, tell yourself that the present is now and the future is then.

149 Live with purpose: a definitive purpose. If you don't, a half-awake corpse remains.

150 Love is an emotion that houses much care, a hearty device with a desirable snare. We can turn around and walk away, or we can embrace love and lead heartbreak astray. Many wish for what is already there, the internal truth in which so many fear. Compassion, warmth, connection and lust, show your affection and disarm your distrust. For this feeling we share is a gift from above, so grasp it tightly and show it your love.

151 Don't place emphasis on what has been and what might be; place emphasis on what is.

152 Happiness. Is it in truth what many of us hope for? Or is it in the answers which happiness may provide? It

is true that many pray for happiness, but such prayer can also be falsified by coinciding thoughts of what happiness actually is. Is it happiness in friendship in which our daily prayer is most directed? Happiness in financial security, and if so, to what end? What about happiness in the development of a certain project – an artistry, of some sort? Maybe happiness comes in the form of an authoritative role? Perhaps it is happiness in the loyalty one shows for their social community? Happiness in the comfort of a close family and retention of a loving partner? Or is it happiness found in the quest for understanding happiness' very eminence? Maybe the pursuit of happiness is more about the pursuit than the happiness itself? Happiness can come in many diverse forms: spiritual; financial (or what is perceived to be); experiencing true love; the ability to provide for your family; appreciating the importance of mortality; in one's professional life; in one's health and vitality; in believing that one believes to be happy. What does happiness mean to you?

Confucius wrote, "The heavens do not say anything." 153 Why would they need to? The heavens' silence tells us so much, but it can only be understood by those who choose to listen. Silence is heavenly. "All of humanity's problems," Blaise Pascal wrote, "stem from man's inability to sit quietly in a room alone." Structuring in some intervals of stillness and silence into your day can do you the world of good. You begin to view the world differently; the trees will whistle for you, the flowers will dance for you, the sky will clear for you and the birds will sing for you. But in order to achieve this higher state of being, we must first learn to become comfortable with being uncomfortable: thinking nothing, saying nothing, doing nothing – positioning ourselves into a state of non-thinking each day whilst sitting in our temple of serenity.

154   If you were to die today, how would you want your friends and family to speak about your life? Would you wish they said you were a hard-working, generous and kind soul who possessed a magnifying energy and an uplifting aura? However you would like to be remembered, start creating the legacy that you'd like to leave behind now, while you still can.

155   Your limitations speak, your potential shines.

156   Is this way of living true to your character or are you in search of another character's approval? Remind yourself, you have lived that way before, in the perception of a perception of yourself, now is the time to put this exhausting way of thinking to rest so you can begin to live for you – because if not you, who? In the words of Charles Horton Cooley: "I am not what I think I am, and I am not what you think I am. I am what I think you think I am."

157   Time has been kind to you; it's now your turn to be kind to it.

158   The only murder that you should commit is the one of your ego.

159   I often find sex to be more convincing of peace than I do sleep. And when I allow myself to wallow on

the thoughts of lust, my sleep becomes hindered. Therefore peace flounders in its purpose. More laborious in emotional toil over the physical exertion sex often demands. Starting now in this very moment, I must avoid, redirect, or courageously banish the onset of sexual desires once and for all. Why so? My mind owns a mood of muddle, my internal compass appears damaged, and the embodiment of self is crying out for salvation. For these reasons, I must, I shall, I will not surrender to sensual temptation, and I will instead take action upon the ambitions that I have set for myself. Victory will prove far sweeter following such a hard-fought battle.

One man be good, another misguided. No man is evil, for evil is a state of the unknown, the unheard, the unseen. 160

It is your faith that acts as the mind's gentle drill-sergeant into helping you to advance to a safer haven of now. When consistently keeping up with faith, not only will you benefit tremendously from your positive daily actions but you will begin to take on an aura of your internal essence like never before. You'll generate the power to gift others with your ambience, supporting a profound transformation in yourself as well as blessing many others with peace, contentment and newly awakened consciousness along the way. 161

In order to move through even the most difficult obstacles in life, one must remember to act in accordance with solutions and not be focused on the orientation of the obstacle itself. Ensuring that 162 you maintain a conscious flow of everlasting faith – in yourself, in the universe, and in the Gods during your daily endeavours, no matter how light or how rigorous they prove – your prayers will always be answered.

163   Do not think or speak ill of death, for death provides a new adventure entirely.

164   Tragedies will occur in life. That's a given. As a result of such inevitabilities, one should not wish that tragic events will not happen as much as one should prepare their minds for how best to manage them for when they do arise.

165   Your satchel is scant of coin, you own no estate nor possess any assets. Am I correct? "You are correct. Though please enlighten me, how does the lack of gold and bricks and land make me less of a man than he who has plenty?" Coins can be difficult to obtain and heavy to carry, yet effortless to spend. The circle of life hums a similar rhythm. Why should we toil so rigorously for something that might be here in abundance today but could quickly translate into a mere memory by this time tomorrow? The farmer will plough his fields until his eyes seal with exhaustion. The blacksmith will weld iron until his hands bleed. The fisherman will aim to catch fish until the ocean eventually catches hold of him. Many will toil until they no longer own a heartbeat, at which point their time on Earth has reached its end. Before one opts to become a slave to their profession, one must ask themselves: for what? If your ambitions are set on acquiring more of this

and more of that for reasons foreign to self, what does that say about you? Are you human or just another object on the marble mantelpiece that you are yet to obtain? Did you believe that a shortage of coin and material possessions would provide me with any less substance in my life than the man who has lots? You stand corrected. I am not just myself, I am not just a human, nor am I solely a man or merely a mortal. I am a thought, a channel of electrifying energies, an origin of art, a single vessel of imagination. I am far more than what meets the eye.

Everything, at one stage or another, eventually comes to an end. The people you meet, the sights you see, the sounds you hear, the memories you share, all of the worldly pleasures and displeasures, all of the emotions that your being embodies, those individuals you charity your time to and those you have stripped time from, all will eventually meet their date with death. My belief is that life and death is merely a thought. An uncommon sphere of deception that guardians tainted fragments of thinking and non-thinking, action and inaction. All that apparently matters and apparently does not matter is the child of the same mysterious nature. It is all in question, and the answer will forever remain disclosed. Leave no room for concern, evil, past thoughts or future speculations, for your time to meet the billions of other men and women who have lived and died before you is fast approaching. Are you ready? You have silenced. Not even a grunt, a sniffle or a whisper. I'm proud of you, therefore I welcome you.

166

167   Become the oak tree that stands its ground even when the most violent of storms blow around it.

168   We all must work. Work to eat, to drink, to sleep, to survive. It is in our nature to do so. Therefore, we should not complain, become flustered or feel dispirited when the time to work arises. A man may grumble that he is fatigued in the morning following a long day of toil the day before, and so rising proves too arduous and it is easier to stay snugly wrapped in his blankets. I am not here to contest that comfort isn't satisfying – it is – but the duty of a human being is not to live in comfort, nor is it to feel satisfied. Such pleasantries are a by-product of the daily obligations which a human is born to fulfil. The internal current that staves off thirst, hunger, frustration, loneliness and depression, work is part of a man's purpose. A purpose of not giving into a life that reeks of inaction in a faculty of wastefulness. The duty of a human being is to do the things that humans were born to do, not to cower away under materials of warmth all day long. Next time when you feel like living a life that mirrors one of a sloth, remind yourself: action keeps us from dying, inaction keeps us from living.

169   Wish not for the evasion of death, but instead, rehearse for its arrival.

170   I apologise for what I have done but I will not apologise for who I have become. Faults during your past times do not have to define you as an individual or your future life. Become a real-life testament of profound change. If the Gods do exist, they would

not have created an opportunity for faults. If the Gods do not exist, then faults have been created by the accordance of the universe, which means it is in our nature to experience such faults. Therefore, if all faults and rightful actions have been created for a specific reason, who are we to question any different?

Life must permit death to define its meaning. Death must enter life to define its purpose. 171

Love. An emotion that can grip and pull on even the toughest of hearts. Love is something we all have inside of us, in which we project upon ourselves in times of despair and in times of great victory. Love stems from an emotional bond between two souls which has the potential to bloom into something beautiful. If love is available for us all to experience, why do so many of us suppress our emotions? Instead of placing a lock around your heart, open up your chest and give your heart the freedom and the opportunity to give love and receive love. Just like the wheels of a bicycle are meant to turn, the strings of our hearts are meant to be played. Do not reject her love, embrace her love and return your love to her. Let Cupid do his job. 172

No wonder you have experienced so many blunders in your past workings – you set yourself another one-hundred-and-one tasks to complete at the same time. You are human, if you needed reminding. Focus on one task at a time. Do not aid concern for past or future happenings during this period. Devote yourself fully to what you are doing at this moment. Go about your task as if it were the only task that you ever had 173 to complete. Once complete, treat every other task that follows in the same way you approached the last. One thing at a time.

174   If you were to receive a slip of paper today that had the exact date and time of your death written on it, how differently would you begin living your life from this moment? Would you make more time for yourself rather than always donating it to others? Would you be kinder and more helpful to those people you come into contact with? Would you love your friends, family and partner more? Would you own a heightened degree of respect for yourself? Perhaps you would spend less time gossiping over trivial matters and focus more of your time on matters of greater significance? Maybe you would like to learn a new language? Write a novel? Travel to a country you've been longing to visit? Perhaps you may finally start that business you've been thinking of for the last five years? If we were all given a slip of paper with the date and time of our deaths, a great deal more humans would be dying happily.

175   Similar to writing, you have the ability to become the meticulous editor of your life. Books are written, books are read. As long as you are writing a book that you would like to read, continue to live your life in the same way.

176   Act now: you will have plenty of time for inaction when you are dead. Until then, be loyal to your beating heart, and live.

Remember this: nature is loaning us this life, so let us   177
not waste the little time it has lent us.

You complain that your morning coffee was not   178
sweet enough, and now your insides are coiling with
vexation for the blunder that the barista has made.
"My morning coffee is ruined," you mutter to yourself.
There is such a thing called human error, I will have
you know. Did you not ever spill milk when you were
a young boy? Rein yourself in, spoilt child, for matters
of triviality are unworthy of such negative energy.
Now, add another sugar to your cup and be done with
it.

You may think the verses you share with others are   179
beneficial to your self-development. But do ask
yourself: for what benefit, exactly? You may think
that the constant interruptions that are vying for your
attention from your smartphone make you a more
connected individual, but this isn't necessarily the
case – and you yourself know full well that it is not.
When a notification presents, the glee you feel is of
falsehood. Indeed, it may excite you and help you feel
valued for a short time, but it's fictional. So, refrain
from breaking that bread, wetting your tongue with
that wine and dancing carelessly around the table, for
the notion of celebration that a small handheld device
grants you is nothing more than a fallacy.

Death victimises nobody – or, you could argue,   180
depending on your outlook, that death victimises
everybody. Regardless of which side of the coin you
may be on, both parties need to realise that death has

been added into each of our lives for one significant reason: to enable us to live.

181   It's busy. It's noisy. I simply cannot concentrate. Amongst the thick fog of life in which you are constantly battling to clear, there is a place that you can travel to which will provide you stillness and muse: your own mind. Ask yourself: do you rush to fill these rare moments of calmness? Do you wish for motion when your body desires stillness? Being silent when sat in a state of stillness is when your being begins to take on a higher power, a deeper meaning and more profound level of consciousness. When you enslave yourself to the hustle and bustle of life, you become nothing more than a half-empty glass of sour milk. Half there, half not. Incomplete and unfurnished. In order to become the person that you were born into this world to be, you must allow yourself to spend quality time in your kingdom of serenity each day. This is where fullness is found.

182   Fault can be found in anything, but good can be found in everything.

183   Worry is an existential response to the initial feeling we impede upon ourselves to experience. It starts out rather minor, then compounds into something that needs to be locked in a cage in order to control. The more we allow worry to circulate inside us, the further we allow ourselves to live with its demonising presence. We find ourselves wide awake in the middle of the night, staring aimlessly at the wall and wishful of rest. We govern ourselves with endless questions:

why did I do that today? Why did I not do that today? What am I doing tomorrow? Why can't I sleep? Where am I? Who am I? More so, one question in particular that we never cease to ask ourselves is one that will always remain unanswered: what is this all for?

Part of your being will always tempt you into betraying your true self, but despite the strength of this relentless enemy of yours, remind yourself that it only has the strength to tempt you, never to push you. 184

Rest with peace. Rise with purpose. March with pride. 185

The best antidote for rejection is acceptance. 186

If your life were to end today, how would you feel about your life? Furthermore, what legacy would live on after you? Would you be just another loose-fitting mortal who once lived in the local hamlet or will you be the one who helped in building the hamlet itself? Would you own the dishonourable status of the mere drop in the ocean or become the embodiment of the ocean as a whole? It is true that many of us want to live a happy life, yet most of us are confused as to what a happy life represents. Many individuals set their ambitions on financial riches yet most are not prepared to put in the work that a life of obtaining financial riches requires. For many others, a question mark remains. When my date with the angel of death arrives, I want to be convinced that I am leaving behind something more than a decaying corpse. I plan to have read thousands of books and written tens of novels that will have a positive impact on an 187 innumerable amount of lives following my departure. You see, whilst it seems that life during our youthful years appeared to be limitless, as we blossom further into adulthood, time is quick to remind us that it is not. Therefore, if every conclusion of a human's life is equal, no matter how good or bad or how long or short a life is, there are no prizes awarded to anybody, for life is a brief moment for all of us.

188 Take some time out of your frantic life and position yourself high up in the sky where you can view your life from a great height. Failing to do so will show injustice to yourself and to others. For how sinful is it that we grant ourselves permission to critique others' good deeds and wrongdoings if we fail to critique our own?

189 Remind yourself of the relic of time equality: a percentage of individuals will live for many joyous years in the shortest lapse of time whilst other individuals will exist in the longest passage of time yet will experience little joy.

190 Billions of mortals have felt the soil beneath their feet before you and billions will tread these grounds long after you are gone. Live for today, or fail to live at all.

191 Do you compare yourself to the millions of leaves dancing on the trees? The millions of waves swishing in the seas? What about the millions of stars glowing in the skies above? "I do not." Well, then, if you do not compare yourself with these worldly creations, why is it that you do so with other humans?

Your mind is the most powerful tool that you possess. 192
It's always the first to arrive at the scene: in danger, in
relief, in happiness, in grief. Your mind is your sight,
your star in the night, your guiding light, your skin
and bones, your ability to fight for what is wrong
and what is right. Be wary of that mind of yours
for it can be your closest ally or your most wicked
enemy; today, it can empower you with joy, but come
tomorrow, it can burden you with sadness. The mind
can affect the heart, too: it can riddle it with haunt
or nurture it with warmth. Be wary of that mind of
yours for it can be the love you crave or the loneliness
you fear. Leverage your mind for beneficial reasons:
to advance the nature of good and to banish the
presence of evil. Be mindful of that mind of yours:
kindness it can find, love it can bind, hearts it can
break, lives it can shake.

Nature: where all comes to live and where all goes to 193
die. A mystic realm where each part of the day that
arrives – dawn, afternoon, dusk – is a child of unity,
a cosmic bond, a gift from Mother Nature. Similar
to each new hour that pays a visit, human life is no
different: a swift departure follows. In life, the young
child is no different to the old man – both stemmed
from the womb of their mother, both on course to
rest beneath the soil, to be turned into ashes or tossed
to the ocean. All lives, be it a short or stretched life,
happy or sad, are equal. All that has been, all that is
and all that is soon to be, is as one.

Do not be impressed by fame or motivated by material 194
gain. In happiness, you should be free of care for the

coins you bear and the clothes you wear. In happiness, you should feel as much fulfilment from a droplet of rain upon your neck as you would by sleeping under shelter each night. Remember: anything more than enough is wasteful, and the wasteful will never have enough.

195   If it has already been achieved by another, it is too within your reach to achieve. He achieved this, she achieved that – you are next in line. A seemingly impossible feat quickly loses its buoyancy when a fragment of action is applied upon it. For the majority of us, as Marianne Williamson wrote: "Our deepest fear is not that we are inadequate. Our deepest fear is that we are powerful beyond measure. It is our light, not our darkness, that most frightens us."

196   Serenity is within you. It always has been. It is often locked up in a dormant part inside your brain. If you have not yet unlocked it, don't settle. Forever continue to explore. You will discover it, eventually. Possession of self, not of any other or any particular thing. Allow yourself to breathe. Do not become the bandit of your own soul.

197   It must be difficult, attempting to remain loyal to your artistry whilst being surrounded by so many temptations. "Attempting!?" Revamp that vocabulary of yours, my friend, as your shortage of ambition does not mirror my own. What about the numerous distractions that you constantly face? "Distractions, being what, exactly?" The babble with others, the lack of muse in the air, the restless flow of social motion.

"Your thoughts are foolish and your verses are biased." How so? "Whilst your limitations speak, my potential shines. In good company, there is love. And with love comes respect. Therefore, the progressions of my aspirations are in full swing, thank you very much. Only in the lack of community I find myself drowning in the devil's spit." So, you are saying that you are more focused on producing your art when there is a shortfall of serenity in the air? "A hut of quietude or a village where the atmosphere is swamped with activity, there is but one parting; it is not in what your entity yearns for but in what your mind requires. You must walk on the path in which your nature demands, be it what you desire most or what you most fear." Please expand. "No difference to a baboon lodging in a tree than a lion seeking shade in a bush. You should harbour no concern or show no pity for he who is performing differently to what you would expect for yourself, for my ambitions are on the cusp of being met."

I am in distress. "Good, now you are finally feeling something real. But do not sit and sulk for too long, for no matters in life are worth burdening your time for any more than is necessary." 198

There is no greater depth that a man can explore than the one in his own mind. Do not come to a conclusion based on what one has said or what one has not said. Travel inside your mind in order to bring about your best judgement call. But do remind yourself that there is no right or wrong in what has been said and what has not been said. 199

200   You purchased that book to place on your shelf – not to read yourself but for others to notice that you own its title. This is your external drowning you out with its perilous current. The side of you which battles against you, never in support of you. This side of you which edges God out instead of standing loyally beside God. Do you really enjoy your art as much as you say you do, or do you enjoy the praise from others that the conclusion of each of your publications provides? To take it a step further, you say you wish to travel the globe to meet new people and to explore unseen sights, but at the same time you mention that you are a practitioner of the stoic philosophy. If I am not mistaken, a true stoic should disengage from the desire in transporting his physical body to anywhere but where he stands tall at present. How so? The stoic has the ability to travel anywhere he likes, whenever and how often he wishes, by travelling inside his mind. Do you contest this? Most unphilosophical of you, then, if so.

201   Not so long ago, I made a conscious decision to stop chasing more in life and instead began pursuing a life of less – applying the power of deliberate subtraction to guide me through. I traded in my miserly aspirations for an artistry that encouraged my creative spirit to waltz. An artistry that would challenge me, provide me with a wellspring of joy, and fill my life with purpose. It is simple in nature, pleasing in execution and grand in conclusion. I have selfishly, and knowingly so, become what I have always desired. And in publication, that desire gleams with great truths. Your art is an extension of your soul.

Abstain from indulging in sexual activity as well as 202
revelling in the thought of it. But, in the unfortunate
event of catching yourself in the act or in thought of
it, conclude and immediately return to your regular
state. Do not carry forward your sexual experience
and share it with any other, or feel it be necessary to
replay the memory back in your mind the same way
you might replay a scene from your favourite movie.
Refrain from subjecting yourself to anything less than
who you are if you have broken your precepts; stand
up straight, listen intently, speak clearly, walk tall and
accept things for what they are. Never allow another
part of your being to surface as a consequence of
succumbing to the goddess of desire. Pay this act – or
thought – no further attention and begin to do what is
right from this moment onwards; staying true to your
internal form and rekindling the energy in which you
have recently exerted. Return to a state of finesse. To
conclude, if your conscience is still feeling somewhat
fractured by your recent relapse, allow me to provide
you with some healing advice that I hope will help you
in returning to your rightful self: human error is of far
greater value than a life free of faults.

Here I lay, huddled under the blankets of my bed 203
whilst reading my book. My body is at rest but my
mind is restless; a battle that I am all too familiar
with. At present, I find myself spectating upon my life
from a great height. I see a young man nestled in his
minimally decorated yet spacious bedroom, wrapped
in warm materials, cosy and content in his abode of
slumber. The young man just lays there, mirroring the

stillness and silence of a monk in a monastery. Not a blink in sight nor a twitch in motion. The muse, the lack of activity, the scarcity of social flow, all appear to be well-tamed to the highest degree in this young man's world. No interruptions. No distractions. Mounted on the wall that overlooks the young man's writing desk lives a shelf stacked with books. His bed, fit for a king, owns the softness of one thousand sheep coats. On his bedside table sits a glass which is full of clean drinking water. Chants of satisfaction are heard within the young man's stomach as his hunger is safely at bay due to the hearty meal he just consumed. His scent, fresh and inviting. His senses, as sharp as a leopard's claw. His hearing, acute. His heart, pure. His vision, clear. His body, strong. The young man has a home to which he occupies these pleasantries, in both the roof that provides him shelter from rainfall and the jacket of flesh that protects his organs. He has the ability to walk wherever he may choose and has been blessed with the gift of speech. The young man's friends are supportive and loyal to him and he is shown love from his family in generous proportion. Furthermore, the young man is not a slave to the system or a prisoner to his country. The young man has his freedom; he is freedom. The young man has more than he could ever want or need. He has enough. What, then, is the reason behind this young man's unhappiness?

204 Many people believe that heaven is above us, but I believe that heaven surrounds us – in close proximity to us. Heaven is never too far away – like the song of a bird, the dance of a tree, the smile of a child. In

death, the dead are not gone; they have simply moved on from their earthly phase of life.

I believe that this life we're living now is one of many, for we are born many times and die many times – countless dimensions of life are experienced, countless times over. Life before life; life after life. When we open ourselves up to the possibility of reincarnation – that we never really die because we are never really born, and that we are never born because we never die – the fear of death diminishes. The life that you are living now, though it may seem challenging to comprehend, is perhaps a sequel from a number of lives you may have lived before. Yes, before this life, you may have lived many other lives. Though it may be difficult to comprehend, there is life before life, and you have lived many times – and once your time in this life expires, you will live again. In-between each one of our lives is a realm where our spiritual self takes rest, a renewal stage in which we become masters of being: silent and still individual entities who reside in an oasis of serenity. During this time, between our last life and our next, is the most important time there is, a time for the regaining of our vital energy in preparation for our next life to begin.

If you ever find yourself feeling anxious or fearful towards your own or a loved one's departure from this life, remind yourself that following this departure, another life lies in waiting. Until that moment, go on dying at the end of each day and go on living at the start of each day as if each day is a new life entirely. Remember, there is no end to life because there is no start to life and there is no start to life because there is no end to life. Life is a timeless loop, ongoing and everlasting. In the consciousness of our eternal life, even death can be beautiful.

205   I'll start by saying this: I have let a great number of people down. Equally, I too have been let down greatly by somebody: myself. All the more foolish, as I have let myself down a great deal more than anybody else. And whilst I am confident to say that I have successfully cleared my conscience in forgiving myself for doing wrong, it would be insincere of me to say so otherwise I wouldn't be writing the words that I am now. Though, in some shallow attempt to justify my defence in the matter, I would claim that a part of me was distant at certain intervals during the undertakings of such injustices. This is not to say that it makes my actions, or lack of actions, pardonable by those who I have let down, including myself – they do not.

206   A true philosopher would never go on blurting out to the crowd that he is a philosopher; a true philosopher would just go about his day in his philosophical way – thinking, reading, writing – allowing his pen to do the talking as opposed to tiring out his tongue. The Gods know who you are and who you are not. The only one who is falling victim to the fool is the man in the mirror. So, then, you must ask yourself: "What, or who, is this all for?" The only way to become yourself is to lose the person you think you are.

207   When it comes to your mind, no matter how far or fast or however long you choose to run for, you will

not ever be able to outrun it – nor will you be able to outwit it. If you are lonely, spending more time in isolation will not help you to feel less lonely. If you're sad, wallowing in the pits of darkness will not help you to feel cheerful. If you're sick and tired of being sick and tired, drowning yourself in complaint of how you're not healthful and sprightly will only deepen your manifestation of such feelings. The key to overcoming these emotional tyrants is to remove yourself from their wretched company once and for all. Theoretically, this may sound difficult. Practically, if you're truly committed to becoming an agent of change, the transition should be seamless.

To do as little as you can, the best you can – because 208
to do everything is to do nothing. Similar to the old and wise words of Seneca: "To be everywhere, is to be nowhere." Therefore, it is important not to spread our time wastefully on meaningless tasks, but to pursue – and complete – a single task at one time, like a professional archer striking a bullseye, doing so with uninterrupted focus and with good aim, and as if that one task was the only task that you were put on this planet to complete.

Your mind is a current; never still, rarely silent, 209
invariably flowing from here to there, and there to the next. In the struggle of attempting to grasp hold of the present moment, place your thoughts upon the king of the jungle: the lion. Do you think the lion has trouble living in the present? No, of course not. If the lion thinks of tomorrow, his today is at risk – he may fall

prey to nature's merciless elements and he, the hunter, will soon become the hunted. There is no other option for the lion but to live presently – moment to moment. The lion does not reflect on yesterday's events either; he does not boast to his pride about how smoothly he took down that buffalo yesterday. In the wild, it is dangerous to have an ego; ego will get you killed. To the lion, today's survival is all that matters. Step by step, kill by kill. If the lion was to reflect on yesterday or speculate on tomorrow, not only would he put himself in grave danger but his cubs and whole pride, too. If the lion does not live in the present, the whole lion species would soon become extinct. For the lion, tomorrow's survival depends on today's efforts.

210 The Gods are always present for man in times of sin or celebration, mania or desperation – for on occasion even the Gods require rest so that they are able to reflect on certain matters of the universe. In the knowledge of this, you will often need to reach out your hand and gently tap the Gods for their shoulders in order to receive the answers to your questions.

211 Men end up resenting themselves for certain disciplines that they have watched slip by the wayside. They punish themselves mentally, physically, and, in doing so, turn themselves inside out emotionally. By laying out the cane for yourself when it is unnecessary to do so, you are showing injustice to yourself – to your human nature, to your internal and external constitution. Go now, grant yourself liberation from the shards of glass that cut into your guilty mind. As

long as you are aware of your doings and undoings, allow your demonising thoughts to fade into the darkness. Remember, nothing that remains undone that can be done is worthy of causing concern.

Just like the bull who stands there tall and strong, doing the job of a bull, I too, as a human being, want to stand content and uncomplaining for what he has, not in frustration for what he has not. 212

For those who fear death, it is not death you fear; the perception you have about death is what you fear. Much like many other things in life, the power of perception is what makes us fearful of the idea of a certain thing, not the thing itself. 213

Do you ever feel like you just want to float away and live up upon the clouds? Where you can escape the chaos of life, where nobody can bother you, a place where you can be alone – where you can live in peace? At present, I feel like escaping. I'm not too sure what I want to escape from, but it's something. Or perhaps everything? As of now, I just don't feel myself. I feel worthless, guilty, full of regret and find myself questioning my entire existence. Despite the sun currently beaming rays of warmth upon my body, I remain cold. My mind feels trapped, almost like I have been caught in a spider's web that I can't untangle myself from. It's not common for me to feel the way I feel at this moment, but every now and then days like today swing by to remind me that, regardless of the intelligence and common sense one may possess, and no matter how many books one reads and the words 214 one writes, life is always going to be in question. I wonder what tomorrow will bring.

215 You must regularly remind yourself that, at this very moment, there are thousands of babies being born into the world; some strong, some weak, some healthy, some ill. Whilst it is fact that all of our days on Earth are numbered, some people will only get to experience life for a few hours, days, months, a couple of years at most – whilst others will be fortunate enough to live for up to one hundred years or more and will have tasted all of the flavours that life has to offer. But even in the case of a newborn baby experiencing life for only a few short weeks, months or years, this is not to say that death is a tragedy – it is not. For the tragedy is in the perception one has towards death, not death itself.

216 Technology allows us to experience the beauty of nature on screen, but to see nature in real life is a different experience entirely.

217 Life will present us with many roads, and when these roads present, they will often reveal themselves in an unpredictable manner. There are no guarantees that the next road we travel on will be straight, promise us any safety or security, or show us any remorse. If you're looking to reach your destination unscathed, you will need to live your life in accordance with your own nature. You must know, as understanding is merely not enough, that you will have to swim through the waters when the ocean's current proves perilous. For this is not how life is won but is how one

can endure life. Life is discovered in the struggle, not in the personal attainment.

Whilst the process of unrestrained expression has been far from fine wine for me at times, my consistency in attendance continues to prove that, in the words of Seamus Heaney, "If you have the words, there's always a chance you'll find the way." 218

I must say, I do find it difficult to be a good man. Which qualities is a good man supposed to carry? Perhaps I'm just less of a man than the average man, or lack knowledge on the difference between being a good man and being good at being a man. Possibly it's down to me being unsure of what type of man I am and how I am supposed to assert my manliness? The answer to these questions remains unknown. 219

Yesterday, I roamed the countryside for several hours with the aim of silencing a few voices in my head. The voices that speak to me when I'm alone. The voices that speak to me when I'm in a crowd. The voices that never allow my real inner voice to have its say. These voices, just like the world we live in, can be loud, busy and manipulative. Your mind is born an individual, but as your mind matures, it becomes less individual. Your mind struggles to find its own voice due to the thick crowd of other voices that it begins entertaining. "Please leave now! You have overstayed your welcome," you may tell the crowd of other voices in your head, but similar to any crowd in need of dispersing, it often takes more than a few words to get them to leave. 220

221 As of today, commit yourself to something bigger than your direct self. Something that will present you with a state of content when your final breath arrives. Something worthwhile, something wonderful, something memorable. Furthermore, something that shows improvement from who you were yesterday and the accomplishments you made last year. Outdo yourself, but in the process of doing so, do not bury yourself.

222 Permit internal order upon yourself or your external self may play foul. The assumptions you have about her act as a boomerang travelling back towards you. Examine yourself with harsh judgement before criticising her.

223 Become so engrossed in your art that you no longer feel the desire to fill your stomach, wet your lips, rest your eyes or indulge in sexual activity. And if you do feel the need to take a timeout away from your art, ensure you do so with good intentions.

224 Today's world is full of mystery; curious at the thoughts of strangers, elated by their actions more than we are of our own. Drama in the fallen world has become our entertainment. We rate it, converse over it, condemn ourselves to it. We are now more drawn to tragic news than ever before. Frightening, indeed – yet we choose not to escape it.

225 Absorb yourself in a bubble of deep concentration where distractions are a thing of the past, a distant

memory. The key to a happy life is to concentrate on what is being done now – the present task at hand, nursing no concern for what the past may have held and accommodating no fear for what the future may bring. In this very moment, put your best foot forward and craft your finest work, and apply all of your magnificent potential to the present moment. Treat each moment as if it were your last.

The ocean can be rough and unpredictable even on 226 the best of days. If you fail to build a sturdy boat, your foundations will begin to crack. After your sail has collapsed and you have lost control of your rudder, your deck will start to fill with water. And eventually, your boat will sink – and you are likely to drown, committing a long and painful suicide.

View yourself as an impermanence – your loved ones 227 too. By doing so, you will love yourself more and cherish the time more dearly with your loved ones whilst you are alive. It is only when we become aware of the angel of death, realising that we can die at any moment, that we become fully aware of the gift of life. The angel of death can teach us many valuable lessons, but the most important being that we may die tomorrow, so we should treat today as if it were our last day to live – and say to ourselves, "There is no tomorrow, there is no tomorrow." Perhaps not too far from now, you, just like me and all of the other humans and animals around you, will experience your initiation with death and have no option but to surrender to it before being laid to rest beneath the soil. I say this not to leave you biting your nails in fear, but only with the intent of bringing you closer to the Himalayas of happiness whilst you are alive.

228 All you do is talk about your work, the money you earn and the material luxuries you possess. Where is the joy in a conversation such as this!? Who cares to open their ears to such nonsense? I find it aggravating to listen to your voice even from afar; I can only imagine the suffering that your own ears must be experiencing right now. The busiest tongue is the worst listener. The active body is the most stressed body. The unrested mind is the most unstable mind.

229 You are just another man who talks about action as opposed to putting any of the words you speak into action. This morning you said, "I'll do it tomorrow." Come tomorrow, you will repeat yesterday's words. You dip your toes in the shallow waters of your work instead of allowing yourself to swim in the deep. What is your reason for not finishing anything you start? You start everything but finish nothing! Is this because you have never truly started something? In this case, the only accomplishment you have attained is the attainment of accomplishing nothing, to which you are prolifically successful.

230 There is no final destination in our journey of life. There is only the journey. You have lived before. Your previous life has been. It has already taken place. The past is past. Now is the time to be present in your current life. This life of yours is now, in the here and now. Do be wary, though, that you do not engross

yourself in the present, for each time you do it is already in the past. When your time to die arrives in your current life, your physical body becomes motionless but your spiritual self lives on – continuing from its earthly phase of life onto the next. Life after life. Our physical body is mortal but our soul is immortal. We are born. We live. We die. Then, we are reborn. Our body will decay and become something of the Earth's matter, but our soul lives on. When we permit ourselves to understand that we are eternal beings, the question we press upon ourselves of how long or short our life will be becomes void – for the life we live is timeless; a state of no-birth and no-death; an everlasting adventure that provides limitless depths in an infinite number of fascinating realms. In order to appreciate and be happy in our current life, we must learn to look beyond our deaths into our next life, as well as speculate upon the possibilities of who we were and what we did in our previous lives – for only then will we pass through to our next life successfully: in acceptance, in peace, in love. Do not fear turning to the next chapter of your life, for it may prove to be the best yet.

To be present, we must focus ourselves – our mind, our body and our spirit on the here and now – on the gift of life: the present. But this gift can be deceiving: it can be the friend that quickly becomes the stranger; it can be the dream that quickly becomes the nightmare. It is the thing we all chase but cannot catch. The present moment is never in our company long enough for us to experience what it actually means and feels like to

231

be in it. The present is here now, at this very moment, and now it's gone. It's here again, and now it's gone again. The present is a repeating loop that never fails to expose its best-kept secret: the present is past. It has already been, it has already gone. Live in the moment but do not get caught up in the present. I write what I have written as if I am the teacher, but how can I be a teacher if I am still flunking in my lessons as a student? In the teachings from Siddhartha Gautama Shakyamuni (the Buddha), "When the student is ready, the teacher will appear." Until then, my battle with the present moment continues.

232　Understand that all that is here today was once not: the oceans we swim in; the mountains we traverse; the animals we eat; and the many men, women and children who live amongst us. All of Mother Nature's creations were nothing before they were something. Life and death are no different. Death is nothing to us for we have been beside it for a great deal of time before we began breathing in this life – therefore you and I, the sand and the ocean, the oak tree and the forest deer, have nothing to fear. If we were to examine death more closely, it would be death that has something to fear, as it is death that has to put up with life, not life having to put up with death. There is a clear start and end to life, just like there is with a novel, a marathon or a man's loving relationship with his wife. What does it matter, then, between he who is born and he who is not?

233　Our prized possessions: our house, our cars, our furniture, our clothes. Who is the rightful keeper of these things? What about our parents, our children – who owns them? Who owns me? There are only two keepers of ownership in this world: life and death. And whichever way you attempt to look at it, time never blunders in exposing the great truth: death brings you life, then you live for a mere moment before death takes you back. All of the things we think we own, as well as the stringent structure we insist to carry in our own lives, are not owned by us or anybody else – the ownership we believe to have is our own self-created fictional perception that we own everything that we don't.

You could be eating a meal or singing a song or making   234
love to your partner. Whatever you are doing at this moment, know that it will be gone in a moment – ensure then that you do it, whatever it is, with totality. This moment is the only moment you have control over. At this moment, when you are wholeheartedly appreciating the single activity you are partaking in, you will experience a certain ecstasy about your life. Your utopia will not be found in ruminating over the past or pondering the future; your utopia can only be found when relishing in the present moment. It is during this present moment that a single second of life can be enough. Another person could live for a hundred years and another person a thousand years and still not experience the same wave of euphoria for their life that you have in that single second. Choose this moment to be alive. Enjoy eating your meal at this very moment, enjoy listening to this song at this very moment, and enjoy making love with your partner

at this very moment – for every other moment is not promised.

235 You have reached peak contentment when you are happy with not living out another day of your life.

236 There is a great number of people who are only content with the utmost in life, but there seems to be few and far between that are content with the opposite: the bare minimum. I, personally, fit into the latter criteria. I am content with very little and desire nothing more than I need to survive; food, water, shelter. Provide me with a new book to read from time to time and a pencil and sheet of paper to write with and I am content beyond the highest degree. To be a stoic in the modern world, one must first own an equal amount of comfort in knowing their death is soon to be upon them as they would take comfort in making love with their partner or taking a walk in the countryside. Until you have accepted that death will not rest until you are within its vices, your life will prove to be an unending tiring ascent towards accomplishing anything worthwhile.

237 It is past midnight and I cannot sleep. This is due to a fellow lodger in the room beside me who is snoring louder than a walrus. "I hope he chokes on his tongue," I whisper to myself with the hope that his doing so will allow me to rest. Now, a mere moment later, I realise that I am putting my hopes of a good night's sleep before someone else's life. Is my 'For me to sleep, he must choke' philosophy really the best approach in this situation? From an outsider's perspective –

one, preferably, who is well-rested – I would beg to differ. A single thought soon befalls me: 'How much of a nuisance am I when I sleep? I may snore, I may wriggle, and I may even talk aloud to myself. What would this man's friends and family think if his death was the result of someone else' wishes for one evening of uninterrupted slumber? Never should I feel like my sleep is more important than another man's life.

During today's walk, I came into contact with a number 238 of different animals. I met a herd of llamas, a tribe of goats, a flock of sheep, a drove of cattle, half a dozen pigs and a string of four horses. As I watched each set of animals closely, it soon became apparent that all these animals shared one commonality: contentment of being. These animals have successfully mastered the art of present living. And there I was, spectating these animals with curiosity, trying to figure out how it was possible for them to be so content with how little they have and how little they were doing. Then it hit me: they are doing what they were born to do. Today's lesson: nothing is harmful to the human condition for the human who is doing what a human is born to do.

Learn to be alone so you don't ever become lonely. 239

I often believe I do certain things for others – not for 240 myself – and this shows injustice within itself. Life is always going to be in question but if we can make clearer sense of who we are, then the world we live in will make more sense too. It starts with you. It ends with us.

241 No better the foot that stands on the soil than the soil that allows the foot to stand on it. No better the bird that perches on the branch than the branch that perches the bird. No better the man who lives in wealth than the man who lives in poverty.

242 Mind, will you ever allow me to be free – to be present, to be me? Free from the uncertain torrents of the future and free from the past that I have already lived. Please liberate me from the cacophony that you continue to rain down upon me. Your presence is as heavy as a gladiator's armour and as sharp as his sword. Ruler of me, my mighty gladiator, before you stick with your blade and observe the blood streaming from my sorry wound, please spare me a few short seconds of this very moment so I know what it feels like to be present for once in my life.

243 Live now in the same way you would wish to live when you leave it; in freedom, unconsumed by worries, untroubled by fears, housing no thoughts for the past or the future – harbouring in the dock of the present moment only, doing so with all of you, because that is all you have. Remind yourself: there is no evil in death, the same as there is no good in life.

244 The death of another – a friend, a family member, a lover, a guardian, a distant relative or a stranger on the street – is not to be grieved over. It should be celebrated. Your mother dies and you say, "I am upset that she is gone." Naturally, as you would be – for your mother has been with you since the beginning of your life. She carried you in her womb, gave birth to you,

nurtured you, has been a mother to you – your mother provided you with the gift of life. For the child that has loved their mother unconditionally whilst she was alive, whilst sadness is a natural emotion to feel, to be distraught over her death is a sin. If, following your mother's passing, you weep uncontrollably, you are saying without saying, "I wish I had loved my mother more and spent more time with her whilst she was alive." Now, a stream of guilt is flowing through you. You have missed the chance to love when love was possible, and now you cannot love as the opportunity to love has been and gone. The death of a loved one is a beautiful thing for those who showed them much love when they were alive. Don't make the mistake of failing to love those whose hearts are open to receive your love whilst they, and you, remain able.

Whether you spend your entire life working towards 245 creating a single masterpiece of art – and you succeed at creating that single masterpiece by the end of your life – or, similarly, if you spend your entire life working towards creating a single masterpiece yet, for whatever reason it may be, you do not succeed in creating that single masterpiece by the end of your life, this too, like the artist who successfully crafted his masterpiece before he was laid to rest, also owns a successful outcome. Both artists lived their lives doing what they loved to do. Their life's purpose has been fulfilled. This is successful living.

Death will arrive and greet each of us, there is no 246 doubt about it. Death is an unquestionable event that nobody can protest against. Even with such stories of those who have claimed to experience the afterlife before returning home seem to lack clarity of their experience. Contradictory to what I have written previously – perhaps due to how I am feeling today as opposed to back then – man cannot guarantee to live another life after this life has passed, and no man can be so sure in his experience that he has lived a life before his life at present. With this, the sole focus should be on living the life that is here, now.

247 We must respect a person's individuality, their independence. If a man chooses to become a monk, this is the man's decision – his own personal decision. Who are you or I to lay judgement upon him or the path in life he chooses to take? The man is now a monk, you are something else, and that is that – so let it end there. We do not judge somebody for what their name is or how old somebody is, so why do we feel the need to judge somebody on what they choose to invest their time into – be it an interest, a profession, or a personal project of some sort? It does not make sense; it is wasteful of time and energy. Therefore, if we value our own time and vital energy, we should not judge anybody – even if somebody has judged us – and if we do find ourselves in a judging match against another, we are deceitful – no better than our opponent for we only end up judging ourselves.

248 Do not try to save the world; only focus on instilling improvement within yourself. Without self-improvement from myself, I cannot reach you.

And if I cannot reach you, you cannot reach the next, and so forth, so the chances of saving humanity become dim. Many people who aim to heal the wounds within humanity often only do so to escape from healing themselves. They possess the healing balm to which they themselves are in need of, but they choose to apply it to somebody else. This is not healing, this is harmful. How does a human save another human who has not yet saved himself? How does a human give love to another human when they themselves are not willing to receive love? It cannot be done. It results in more bad than good, more pain than comfort. To save others, you must first save yourself. Individual by individual; this is the way humanity can be saved.

Monday. Next week. Next month. Next year. That's when I will begin. That's when I will begin to write my novel. That's when I will quit drinking. That's when I will begin to spend more time with my children. But until then, I can't begin. I can't begin because I don't have the time. I can't begin because I am tired. I can't begin because, well … Why can't I begin? 249

When you take a walk in the woods, you are greeted by many trees towering above you and many flowers dancing around you, but what you see you choose not to see. You may say to yourself, "That sure is a magnificent looking tree" and "What a beautiful flower that is", but that is the end of the line for your gratitude toward the tree and the flower. You cease to allow your shallow curiosity of an element of nature to bloom into something of greater meaning. You say: 250

"Whatever they are and wherever they be, they are just there – a tree is a tree. Nothing inherently bad about it, nothing inherently good about it." So, are you saying that a flower is just a flower? An animal is just an animal? A human is just a human? Whilst you may notice and respect a human's external features – their gender, their skin colour, the clothes they wear, the way they walk and the way they talk – you fail to let your dismal level of interest to compound into something more: what the person's name is, how the person thinks, what their interests are, where their values lie. Who the person really is. The reason for you not taking the time to explore a creation of Mother Nature further, and in more depth, is because deep down on a subconscious level, you are fearful that you may understand a tree, a flower, an animal or another human better than you understand yourself. If you can learn to develop the art of caring for all of Mother Nature's creations as much as you care for yourself, a walk in the woods will never be the same again.

EPILOGUE

"Dwell on the beauty of life," Marcus Aurelius wrote. "Watch the stars, and see yourself running from them."

As an extension of the gratitude I bear for all of Mother Nature's creations, and as a token of my appreciation for the world that I have been fortunate enough of being born into, I would like to continue on with my rain of gratitude in thanking you, dear reader, for taking the time to read this book.

Initially, I did not set out to write a book. As selfish as it sounds, I had no desire to help anybody else but myself. "How are you able to help another," I often wondered, "if you have not first helped yourself?" It cannot be done, was the answer that routinely followed. Armed with this compelling insight, and as my alcohol-riddled body pined for sobriety and my puzzled mind wept for solution, I opened up my heart and began bleeding words onto paper until I had but little blood left to give. And then I bled some more.

When I first adopted the habit of daily writing, towards the tail end of 2017 when I was twenty-five, the act was as equally foreign to me as attempting to learn German. Thank you, but no thank you. Or should I say, *Danke, aber nein, danke*. During the three-year period it has taken me to write this book, there were times when I wanted to run away and never return. Sometimes the words flowed as effortlessly as a warm breeze on a summer's day. Other times, the blank page appeared undefeatable, as if I was a legion of one preparing to wage war against a three-hundred-strong army of Spartan warriors. But similar to any other practice that one fully devotes themselves to, as Jenny Saville, the contemporary British painter, wrote: "If there is a wart or a scar, this can be beautiful, in a sense, when you paint it."

Fortunately, offering merit to the power of faith, I was able to drown out self-doubt and replace it with self-confidence and purge any lingering procrastination attempts before relighting the flame of productivity inside of me. Faith power has proven time and time again to be an astounding support system to me in times when I found myself nearing the edge of emotional bankruptcy. By writing out my thoughts on paper – having to regularly force myself to tap into the deepest recesses of my mind, where my darkest thoughts lie and most haunting memories reside – and after numerous hard-fought months of wrestling with the blank page, I was eventually, and thankfully, able to put pen to paper and allow my most troubling thoughts to roam freely. And even though the act of writing was a far stretch from the art of writing during this period, as peculiar as it is, the beauty in denouement pales in comparison to the process of what was.

I encourage you to consider employing your own daily expression practice as you move ahead with your life. Your expression can take shape in a number of forms: singing, dancing, painting, poetry, playing a musical instrument, performing in the theatre, and many more. The choice is yours, and your choice is magic. By adopting a daily practice of your own, doing so will not only support you in dusting off the cobwebs of certain dormant parts of your brain, but it will also allow your eyes to see more, your body to feel more, and your heart to love more, gifting you with a new perspective on all of which you think, say and do in your life, leading you to live each day as if it were a new life entirely.

FURTHER READING

As a token of my appreciation in recognising that my life wouldn't be what it is today without the books that I have been fortunate enough to read, I would like to take this opportunity to share with you ten books that have not only stimulated my intellect and nourished my soul, but also helped me become a better human being:

1. Harry Potter and the Philosopher's Stone by J. K. Rowling
2. The Power of Positive Thinking by Norman Vincent Peale
3. Many Lives, Many Masters by Dr Brian Weiss
4. Man's Search for Meaning by Viktor Frankl
5. Diary of a Young Girl by Anne Frank
6. The War of Art by Steven Pressfield
7. The Last Lecture by Randy Pausch
8. Meditations by Marcus Aurelius
9. Fight Club by Chuck Palahniuk
10. Letters from a Stoic by Seneca

For a list of other books that have had a profound impact on my life, you can sign up to my reading list at ChrisJonesBlogs.com/bookclub (it's free and comes with a No Spam Guarantee!).

Everything that remains can be found on my blog: ChrisJonesBlogs.com

EVERYTHING THAT REMAINS

Writing is a tough gig. Writing can be tough on the best of days, but it can become especially tough when you have a crowd of other voices in your head telling you to put down the pen and go party instead. And writing becomes extra tough when you allow for a gang of technology gadgets to sit beside you vying for your attention every eight seconds, seven seconds, six seconds. I have lived as a cyber-zombie in the past, where my phone became more important to me than my parents, and social media became my newly preferred drug of choice. I was a media addict, and Facebook was my crack. I hated the person I was pretending to be back then, but I love who I am now: the individual in real life, not the prisoner locked up behind those four glass walls who was existing in a world of falsehood. Never will I return to such a lifeless state of non-being. Not in this life or the next.

As you may have imagined, I don't have Facebook or Instagram or Twitter. And no, I don't have Snapchat or Tinder or any other social applications. I don't even own a smartphone, or any phone for that matter. Gosh I feel so free.

After much time debating whether or not I actually need an email address, I have decided to take at least some level of communicative responsibility and maintain ownership of one – at least for the time being, that is. So, if you do insist on contacting me, please note that the email provided below is the only way to do so – unless you feel compelled to take a trip to Wales and knock on my door, to which I would be more than happy to welcome you in, pour you a nice cup of tea and discuss with you the matters at hand.

Email: christopherjoneswriting@gmail.com

Please note: If and when you do decide to contact me, please ensure that before doing so, your body is well-rested and that your mind is at ease. Please also remind yourself that my time is equally as valuable as yours is. I would never attempt to disrupt your precious family time by calling at eight o'clock in the evening to pose you a question that I wasn't able to get the answer to on Google in three seconds flat. Therefore, I politely ask you to treat my time with the same respect as I would yours. With this in mind, please make your airmail inquiry conducive otherwise I will not respond. Thank you, and good day.

ABOUT THE AUTHOR

Christopher Eric Jones is a recovered alcoholic and drug addict turned fitness coach turned plutomaniac turned writer.

As you are soon to find out, Christopher is no stranger to the school of hard knocks. After being removed from two educational institutions (secondary school and college) in his mid-teenage years due to "inexcusable behaviour", he began job-hopping as if job-hopping was his actual job, and soon began experimenting with alcohol and drugs in search of life's answers – eventually leading Christopher down a painstakingly long four-year road of battling his addictions. During these dark and seemingly hopeless times, he wished that his death would amount to more than his life. It was at the height of his addictions that he committed to transforming himself from a catalyst of self-destruction into an agent of positive change. From there, without admittance into rehabilitation nor through the support of his friends and family (mainly, because they were unaware of how turbulent his life had become), and with nothing short of a miracle, Christopher managed to break free from the curse of addiction and began a new life somewhere far away from home, where he went on to gain employment with a well-established health and fitness company working as an exercise coach.

Following four years of working in the field of health and fitness, Christopher had grown sick and tired of the industry he once loved. Whilst seeking other avenues to pursue, he spotted an opportunity on the internet which presented huge potential to create a fountain of wealth for himself by selling consumable products (setting his sights on nutritional supplements and coffee beans) on a well-known multi-billion-dollar online marketplace.

But then, after three years within the unrelenting world of business bringing all of his miserly aspirations into fruition, a rather unfortunate series of events began to unfold. Christopher – then twenty-six years old and in possession of many material luxuries, due to the greedy habits he had started to adopt as a result of having more money than he knew what to do with – had become the individual he once wished he would never become: a narcissistic asshole. The transition from the once kind-hearted and generous young man into the poster-boy of consumerism was soon to provide Christopher with the wake-up call he was in dire need of.

As Christopher watched his business slip into the gallows and his prize possessions get repossessed, now on the cusp of financial bankruptcy and emotional collapse, burdened with a multitude of financial complications and legal repercussions to contest with, it wasn't long before he found himself contemplating relapse. Moments prior to doing so, Christopher first decided to dust the cobwebs off his once cherished journal, picked up a pen and started to write down his most troubling thoughts inside it – as he had done religiously before whilst encountering previous obstacles. Fortunately, Christopher never did take the drug or pick up the bottle that day; instead, he reintroduced the thrill of daily writing into his life, which would yet again go on to fill his heart with warmth, his soul with joy, and his life with purpose.

Now five years clean and sober at the age of twenty-eight, Christopher resides in a quaint countryside village in Wales, in the United Kingdom, with his family. His interests include reading books, writing down whatever springs to mind, drinking coffee, eating pizza, circuit training, enjoying long walks in the countryside, taking naps and spending time with his close circle of friends and certain members of his family. Christopher no longer drives a car or owns a television, doesn't have social media (he doesn't even own a mobile phone), and has a terrible credit score. Christopher is now sitting down at his desk writing his latest book.